DOG RELAX©

relaxed dogs, relaxed owners

Sabina Pilguj

Hubble & Hattie

Hubble & Hattie

For more than eighteen years, the folk at Veloce have concentrated their publishing efforts on all-things automotive. Now, in a break with tradition, the company launches a new imprint for a new publishing genre!

The Hubble & Hattie imprint – so-called in memory of two, much-loved West Highland Terriers – will be the home of a range of books that cover all-things animal, produced to the same high quality of content and presentation as our motoring books, and offering the same great value for money.

Translated by Anna McLuckie

First published in October 2010 by Veloce Publishing Limited, Veloce House, Parkway Farm Business Park, Middle Farm Way, Poundbury, Dorchester, Dorset, DT1 3AR, England. Fax 01305 250479/e-mail info@veloce.co.uk/web www.veloce.co.uk or www.velocebooks.com. ISBN: 978-1-845843-33-5 UPC: 6-36847-04333-9 Originally published in 2009 by Müller Rüschlikon Verlag, Stuttgart, Germany.

Readers with ideas for books about animals, or animal-related topics, are invited to write to the editorial director of Veloce Publishing at the above address.
British Library Cataloguing in Publication Data – A catalogue record for this book is available from the British Library. Typesetting, design and page make-up all by Veloce Publishing Ltd on Apple Mac. Printed in India by Replika Press.

Contents

Acknowledgements

I would first like to say a big thank you to my three very patient dogs, who were always happy to have their photos taken. I was particularly moved by Santino's stamina: he had only recently arrived in Germany, severely traumatised and fearful of all human contact. He now loves massages so much that he demands them frequently. He was very patient and allowed himself to be photographed time and again, never showing any signs of stress and always enjoying his tasks. All three dogs seemed really absorbed in their 'modelling' and had to do without me for a while as I have been working on two book projects at once.

Amigo, Benji and Santino, you are simply wonderful dogs – thank you.

I would like to express my deepest admiration for and thanks to my son, Ricardo (pictured opposite, with my dogs), who is responsible for the beautiful photos. He has taken up photography only relatively recently, teaching himself to use photo editing software on the computer. He contributed so many great ideas and suggestions to this project, and kept providing me with inspiration; his contribution to this project has been really professional. I am very proud of you, Ricardo.

I would also like to mention my husband, Frank, who gives me the space for my projects and is always there with advice when I need it, particularly when I have got into a grammatical tangle. Thank you for your support in all areas of my life.

A big thank you to Dr Ursula Zimmerman, vet and kinesiologist from Lüneburg. As a vet with an holistic practice, she was immediately taken with the Dog Relax project, and was always ready to share her knowledge with me when needed.

Many thanks to vet Christiane Krüger who sent me the valuable treasure of the diagram of the ear from the book *Auriculotherapy on animals* (Christiane and Dr Hartmut Krüger), and gave me permission to use it. The recommendation that I contact her came from Dr Draehmpaehl.

Thank you very much to Andres Gehrdau (visualisation of communication), and Elisabeth Schütz (yoga exercises in the Windlicht in Handorf).

Thank you to all the other helpers who have assisted me with technical matters to do with physiotherapy, osteopathy, singing bowl massage, and kinesiology.

My heartfelt thanks to Tanja Askani for the moving moment of communication between arctic wolf and Podenco in the wild, and for her permission to use the photo.

I would also like to thank Jaume. He enabled me to observe co-existence in a dog pack and how Podencos function together in a group. I am proud to report that my Spanish friend loves his group of over 30 Podencos more than anything else.

The cast
Amble, Border Collie bitch
Anka, Sheepdog/Doberman cross
Baily & Phyllis, mongrel puppies, originally unwanted but now happily re-homed

Bella, English Setter bitch
Charly, mongrel
Celia, Podenco cross
Chira, Bergamasco Sheepdog
Elko, Terrier cross
Elsa, Irish Wolfhound puppy (15 weeks old)
Fluse, Podenco/Ibicenco bitch
Ghalah, Collie bitch with puppies from the Collies von den Dörnbergwiesen kennel
Josie, the brown Galgo
Justy, brown Greyhound
Kia, Retriever bitch
Maggy, Irish Wolfhound bitch
Pierro, Spanish Pointer
Pintat and the other Spanish Podencos
Scally, Labrador cross
Teddy, the black and white Border Collie
Tristan (brown and white), and Tolstoi (black and white), the Papillon brothers
Zissy (known as Ronja), chocolate Labrador

My thanks to these and all the other dogs who were photographed for this book.

Foreword

by Dr Ursula Zimmerman

Something we often ask each other is "How are you?" And not infrequently the reply is "Really stressed at the moment!" Stress is something that is common for humans, but I wondered if animals also suffer from stress: the answer to that is a resounding "Yes!"

In my veterinary practice, I have conversations with dog owners which tell me time and time again that both human and dog demonstrate the same reactions to stress. For example: irritability, susceptibility to illness, excessive increase in or loss of appetite. It is an obvious and incontrovertible fact that dog and human live closely together and communicate constantly. Out of all our companion animals, the dog has the closest emotional bond with humans, and even adopts the same emotional state of his carer. If the human is suffering from stress, then his dog probably is, too; if one of the two is in a state of imbalance, then the other one doesn't feel too good either.

Recognizing this helped me move toward more holistic practice; not just looking at the symptoms of an illness, but also considering the broader picture of the dog/owner scenario. In the human/dog relationship, the two form a unit comprising many facets which are constantly changing, so it is important that I find out as much about the current living situation and state of health of the dog owner, in order to determine how best to proceed to heal the dog (and maybe also the owner!), although it is, of course, far preferable to prevent the illness in the first place with proactive preventative care.

Huge technical advances have been made in both human and veterinary medicine, but I believe that still too little attention is paid to the psychological state of the patient. Symptoms of illness are signals for the body to begin fighting whatever ails it; the view that forms the basis of holistic human and veterinary medicine. Dr Samuel Hahnemann, founder of homeopathy, and the English founder of Bach Flower Therapy, Dr Edward Bach, were convinced that: "There is no such thing as illness, only ill people. Illness is neither an atrocity nor a punishment, but a tool which our soul uses to alert us to our own mistakes." So recovery is always dependent on becoming more self-aware and on assuming responsibility for oneself and an animal.

In order to prevent an illness in the first place, my experience has led me to form the opinion that it is important to constantly work to keep a harmonious balance between the physical, emotional, and mental states.

Our objective should be to behave responsibly towards ourselves and our fellow companions, regardless of species. Our dogs have their own level of consciousness which they can use to develop and blossom, insofar as they are allowed to; each has certain options in terms of which way he wants his life to go. If a human limits him too much in this respect, it can result in behavioural disturbances, neuroses, or unpredictable reactions. In other words, we have to learn to meet our dogs' needs appropriately. In turn, this demands that we are straight with ourselves and don't exploit the dog for our own spiritual wellbeing; instead, taking this opportunity to work on developing ourselves alongside our canine partners in order to experience both joy and relaxation.

Sabina Pilguj – who has worked for many years as an animal psychologist, alternative therapist and yoga teacher – has written a book containing a wealth of experience in relation to

How each to the whole its selfhood gives, one in another works and lives!
How Heavenly forces fall and rise, golden vessels pass each other by!
Blessings from their wings disperse: they penetrate from Heaven to Earth,
sounding a harmony through the Universe!
From Goethe's Faust

the relationship between animals and people. She always takes an holistic approach in her work, sensitively leading us to an appreciation of the importance of enabling both ourselves and our four-legged friends to find peace and tranquillity away from the stresses of everyday life, at the same time, encouraging the reader to encompass a more integrated view of the human/dog relationship.

As a vet with an holistic approach to animal medicine, I am pleased to recommend a book that contains simple, practical, integrated exercises which will improve your dog's wellbeing, giving you the chance to consolidate your relationship with him through health-promotiong massage and physical exercises (easily incorporated into everyday life). The exercises provide a beneficial stimulus for healing "illness," and are naturally even more important in the prevention of illnesses as they help restore the harmonious relationship between physical, mental and emotional states (known as homeostasis), and unite them as an integrated whole.

Preface

Dogs are our four-legged friends. We have an obligation to ensure that they are happy and fulfilled on both mental and physical levels, as well as sufficiently challenged and stimulated. The concept of Dog Relax is not meant to replace standard dog training or physiotherapy as prescribed by a vet. The suggestions in this book have been carefully tested by me, but every human and every animal is an individual, and can experience disparate reactions to different stimuli. Neither the publisher nor myself can provide an absolute guarantee of the effectiveness and safety of the practical application of the suggestions and exercises within the book.

Please consult a doctor or vet if you have concerns, and note that sick or injured animals should not be massaged or moved without having first consulted a vet. Special care must also be taken in the case of pregnant bitches.

Over the many years that I have been working in this field, the connection between stress and its physical and psychological effects on people has become more and more obvious to me. These days, children are particularly strongly affected, and it is horrifying to note that evidence of the full range of psychosomatic, stress-related illnesses can now often be seen in primary school age children. These include symptoms such as tension headaches, stomach aches, agitation, problems with concentration, anxiety, and depressive episodes.

As stress affects both adults and children, it must also be having some kind of impact on our pets, especially since it has been proved that our stress can have an effect on the mood of our animals.

We can always attend relaxation classes, and let go of our worries and tension. But what is available for our best friend, the dog? Virtually nothing which will help dogs find peace and relaxation; on the contrary, it is taken for granted that dogs will support us through the trials and tribulations of our lives. Dogs take part in a variety of sports activities to ensure they are working to full capacity; others are primped and preened, and expected to behave superbly on every occasion. If a dog doesn't behave as humans expect them to, an appointment is made with a 'dog therapist,' who will endeavour to help the dog 'behave' again. However, the dog's own needs are often barely taken account of, and his opportunities for expression either overlooked or simply ignored. A dog is not a machine, but a living creature who still carries within him the imprint of his ancestor, the wolf. We humans don't have the same feelings each and every day, so why do we expect our dogs to?

Our children today have very high expectations placed upon them. It doesn't take much for them to be labelled hyperactive, and even to be prescribed medication in an effort to get them to 'function' again. It's a very similar scenario for the dog: if he doesn't 'function' according to society's standards, he is quickly labelled hyperactive, or said to have behavioural problems. As a result, his needs and breed-specific traits are often overlooked.

A town-dwelling Border Collie who has been acquired as a family pet and companion sometimes seems uncontrollable. However, this dog is not hyperactive and behaviour therapy is not going to help him. This breed of dog is genetically unsuited to the life of a lapdog; he needs plenty

Dog Relax®
www.hunde-helfen.de
Coaching für Mensch und Hund
Spiel & Spaß für Windhunde und Podencos

What is happening with the world today? We live in fast-paced, noisy, hectic times; we can't stop this or turn back the clock, but, in order to survive, we have to learn to find time for peace and relaxation.

Communication between an arctic wolf and a Podenco Ibicenco.

of physical and mental stimulation and activity. The Border Collie is bred to be extremely aware of its surroundings, so a walk through a city can mean that he is bombarded with stimuli. How can he process this?

And it's not just Border Collies that are kept in conditions inappropriate to their breed ...

Sadly, dog owners often don't realise that their dog is uncomfortable. I have intensively studied this subject for several years, and have found that much of what helps humans deal with stress can also be used on our dogs.

Amble, focusing.

The Dog Relax concept

"If you show a dog you love him, he will reward you with an abundance of unconditional love every day." – Sabina Pilguj

og Relax is something that developed out of my own experience and out of necessity. I wanted to use my young dog as a 'co-therapist' in my work, but he, unfortunately, had a traumatic experience at dog training classes. As a consequence, my dog, who, up until then, had always loved all other dogs, now became nervous and uncertain when he was on the lead, and was more and more aggressive towards other dogs. When he behaved like this, I noticed that I also felt more and more uncertain and stressed, mainly because around that time there had been a lot in the media about a dog attack and I didn't want my dog's behaviour to reflect badly on all dogs.

With hindsight, I can see that my body language, thoughts and uncertainty (and increased stress hormones), made my dog so unsure that he carried on with this unusual behaviour almost in self-defence, feeling that he couldn't rely on me to be his 'pack leader.' (This is not the best term to use in relation to behavioural biology, and not entirely correct, either, as our domestic dogs don't live in a pack, but in a family group. However, in the context of my explanation, I think the description of myself as pack leader is very apt.)

Humans learn and grow from encountering problems and mistakes: my dog's lead aggression meant I had to find a way of dealing with his behaviour. None of the dog training schools I visited offered me any help with this, all seeming, instead, to be more concerned with teaching basic commands (which is why, if you want to find a school, you should visit several different dog training classes to evaluate the trainers and their teaching methods).

With hindsight I can see that several months of attendance at traditional dog training classes were not as useful as, for example, a few intensive sessions with skilled and well known dog experts might have been. This was what first enabled me to realise how fascinating it can be to motivate

The message here is quite clear!

dogs correctly, observe communication and body language in detail (eg by using film analysis), and learn to understand them. When the experts demonstrated to me the subtle shades of meaning in canine communication, I felt as if I was discovering a whole new world. And, of course, I wondered why the dog training classes that I had attended weren't passing on this kind of information, or teaching these principles, because they are essentially the prerequisites of a good relationship with any dog! Thankfully, recent years have seen many changes for the better.

Armed with new knowledge, I was able to build a more intensive relationship with my dog and develop a new basis for trust. During the process, I became ever more conscious of my thoughts, and expression thereof, and the significance of this in dog training. I noticed that when I wasn't quite on the ball intellectually, my dog reflected this and was less attentive.

I also became much more sensitive in my awareness of other dogs: it made me really sad to see confused dogs being dragged into noisy cafes; likewise, the bullied victims of 'canine louts' in parks, the owners quite convinced that the dogs were 'playing' happily, even though one was lying whimpering on the ground. Dogs such as these aren't enjoying their time at the park, but are suffering enormous stress!

An intensive course with Amelia Kincade – author and trainer: *Straight from the horse's mouth, communication with animals* – gave me a deeper insight to the emotional world of dogs. I observed how dogs are 'trained' using rigorous and severe methods – pulling their ears, throwing ridiculous rattling tins at them, poking a finger in their ribs, and that kind of thing. Some of these dogs never received any praise at all.

A training regime with no positive affirmation means that the dogs are constantly under stress. Seeing people treat their dogs this way left me speechless, because, of course, a dog is a sentient being with a soul.

"The single worst thing you can do to an animal is to make it feel afraid." – Temple Grandin, 2007

Thanks to the biologist Marc Bekoff from the University of Colorado in Boulder, and the research that he carried out into a variety of animals (including dogs), over a thirty year period, it is now beyond any doubt that animals have feelings. ("There is no question whether animals have feelings.")

Antonio Damasio, an American neuroscientist, says: "Emotions may already have occurred in the evolutionary process in non-human species." I think most owners would agree that dogs

have emotions, and that they can also perceive our emotions and feelings. Every dog owner has undoubtedly experienced how emotions and moods can be transferred from the dog to the owner and vice versa.

For example, a dog that is usually very confident becomes uncertain in a test situation, as his master has suddenly been gripped by exam nerves and the dog has sensed this. You will probably also have experienced someone yawning very obviously, whereupon you feel the need to yawn, too. Or, you watch a sad film and then find yourself feeling down. This mirroring is the result of stimulation of our mirror neurons.

"A mirror neuron is a neuron that fires both when an animal acts and when the animal observes the same action performed by another. Thus, the neuron 'mirrors' the behaviour of the other, as though the observer were itself acting." – Wikipedia

Identified in the mid-1990s by Giacomo Parma, scientists have discovered that these mirror neurons form the basis for intuition and empathy. As described by Joachim Bauer, it is not merely the gesture or expression that can be propagated but also the feelings associated with the gesture or expression. All our behaviours and attributes – such as physical expression, gestures, voice, eye contact – and our actions elicit a range of mirror reactions in others. The existence of these mirror neurons in autistic people is currently unproven, and research continues to determine whether this may be the reason why showing empathy is difficult for those suffering from this condition. Monkeys have been found to have mirror neurons, and , according to Joachim Bauer, dogs also share this phenomenon, demonstrated by the mirroring that occurs between human and dog.

"Species which can mirror each other form friendly cross-species liaisons." – Joachim Bauer 2006

A fascinating study by Kun Guo and his team discovered that when dogs look at people, they tend to look at the right side of the face, a phenomenon known as the 'left gaze bias,' or LGB, and not only dogs do this but humans do, too. The latest research indicates that human emotion is expressed more clearly on the right side of the face than on the left; Kun Guo's theory is that dogs use LGB in order to quickly determine a person's mood. When gazing at inanimate objects, dogs do not have a preference for which side they look at; LGB is something they use with humans only.

The human brain comprises two halves, and each has different functions: the left hemisphere is used for rational processes such as language and calculation, whilst the right hemisphere is responsible for our creative and artistic output. I have wondered for some time whether this is the same with dogs, but so far this has not been proven.

In addition to having to grapple with all of our many incomprehensible emotions, dogs also have to process a host of different sources of stress such as noise, hectic activity, and excessively high expectations on the part of their owner. Also, dogs often experience too little in terms of genuine recreation and species-appropriate activity.

A puppy should be exposed to as many environmental stimuli as possible right from the start in order to ensure that he will grow into a well-balanced, well-socialised adult dog, but a puppy that is dragged for hours around a busy market is under far too much stress for a young dog. Puppies need a healthy balance between activity, contact and rest periods.

I believe that these days very many dogs suffer with acute stress, either from being over- or under-challenged or because of a lack of understanding on the owner's part. In the worst case scenario, this can result in the animal behaving aggressively.

"Anyone who wants to see the true nature of the dog, must transfer to the dog all the qualities presented by poets and thinkers as being the absolute best in human nature. The dog is a very social animal; much more social than humans, but this also makes him more sensitive, more vulnerable, and therefore also prone to contrary reactions." (Trummler, 2004)

Dogs sometime behave in a way that attracts attention, but this does not mean that they have behavioural problems. Every dog owner needs to wake up and look at his dog from a new perspective in order to be able to understand his behaviour, which would provide the stimulus for a rethink on the way we deal with dogs.

I have very often seen dogs in a stressful situation whose behaviour could be quickly changed by some simple massage, and, encouragingly, I have heard from dog lovers that more and more people are taking their pets for physiotherapy to increase the wellbeing of their animal.

Dog Relax is an approach that sometimes works small miracles

I began to observe my own dogs. I wanted to know what helped them relax, which movements they loved and which movements they regularly do themselves. I found out from vets and veterinary physiotherapists what is beneficial for canine musculature.

As a lecturer and teacher, I have had more than 20 years in which to gather a wealth of experience on the subject of stress reduction. I am a great fan of acu yoga, which entails using physical movements to stimulate certain meridians and acupressure points, thereby doing something good for your body. At some point I began to transfer my experiences and observations to the human/dog team and to work on developing a concept.

I have adapted all my experiences from training and further education in the areas of movement, stress reduction, yoga and relaxation, clinical psychomotor issues, kinesiology (*Tree in One, Health Kinesiology*), acupressure and massage to focus on the human/dog team. My aim is to provide carefully targeted relaxation techniques for both human and dog.

The human needs to learn to use movement and breathing to relax when he is with his dog, and to develop new inner strength. A relaxed person radiates calm and clarity, which is very different from a stressed person's aura. Furthermore, the human should learn to develop awareness of his dog's needs and how to understand them.

The dog will benefit from different movements, which will relax the musculature by way of lengthening, stretching and special key exercises; a gentle, playful way of showing the dog how movement can calm him.

Doing these movements together strengthens your bond and mutual trust.

I am not a 'dog trainer' with a new training method (there are already more than enough of those), but regard myself as a relaxation coach for people with dogs!

This marvellous fusion of communication and relaxation between human and dog with wellbeing massages for the dog (which aren't just of benefit to the dog), is a method and technique that I have called 'Dog Relax.'

Dog Relax©

My dog & me

A dog may be our companion, but we should not anthropomorphize her. Behaviourist Eberhard Trummler wrote that this is dangerous, because an animal lover thinks differently to those people who exaggerate their love for animals into something human.

"Humans can probably still be said to be all animal, but animals are definitely not all human."
– Konrad Lorenz, 2004

A dog is a dog and needs to be respected as such! We humans can ensure that our four-legged friends remain healthy. However, the greatest proof of love is demonstrated by how much we respect our dog for what she is.

Even if you are strongly motivated to undertake everything together with your dog, and always want to have her close to you, I would ask you to remember that she has her own needs. In earlier times, dogs had a job to do, and were physically fully stretched as a result. These days, many animals are kept as pets and companions, in order that their owners can satisfy their own need for love and closeness. It is commonly believed that a dog must be happy because she receives plenty of love and attention, and gets a treat from time to time. But if you're honest, you undoubtedly don't like being constantly fussed over or touched and prattled at all day by someone; it would certainly make me feel like my head was going to explode! Constant petting or constant chatter can make a dog very stressed and unhappy. Learn to rein in your need for cuddles in order to ascertain what your dog's real needs are (I'll be addressing this later). She may look sweet and cuddly, but she still has a large proportion of wolf in her, with all the associated ancient instincts. Let your dog be a dog and not a surrogate partner or child.

Sometimes, less is more. Show your dog love and give her attention in a controlled way. A dog needs quiet times and a place of her own where she can rest and sleep undisturbed.

Are you motivated to begin the Dog Relax programme and massages? Then, first of all make sure you pay careful attention to your dog's moods.

If you have a very nervous or traumatised dog, you will need a very sensitive approach.

I can only provide general guidelines here, so please bear in mind that every dog is UNIQUE, and requires a very individual approach that may sometimes call for a great deal of patience, consideration, and understanding.

SHOWING STRESS THE RED CARD
Less stress = more enjoyment for humans & dogs!

The adverse effect of stress on humans is scientifically proven, but stress is not restricted to those in managerial positions, as recent studies have shown that housewives suffer from stress and burnout syndrome, and it has also been proved that dogs – and other animals – also suffer hugely from stress.

Dogs are highly social animals with a very keen sense of perception, which means they quickly pick up on any worries that their human may have. Simply living with a stressed person causes the dog an enormous amount of stress: less stress, therefore, means more enjoyment of life for dog and owner.

Let yourself be motivated to begin Dog Relax, and learn to be precisely aware of your dog's behaviour.

Dogs owned by hyperactive people demonstrate very similar behavioural patterns. With anxious or overly cautious owners, dogs can also exhibit signs of anxiety, which can sometimes be masked by nervous aggression.

To enable us to reduce our dog's stress levels, we often have to alter our own behaviour.

A stressed person is not completely in control, which will cause the dog to feel anxious and uncertain. Raised levels of stress hormones over the long-term can, depending on the constitution of the individual, have consequences for health. In some people, stress shows itself in the form of headaches, stomach aches or diarrhoea, depending on the individual's physical weak spots. A stressed person will sometimes speak more loudly, which also results in the dog being more excitable and therefore stressed.

Agitation and stress are psychological burdens for humans and dogs. Raised levels of cortisol (the stress hormone) impede learning, as the cortisol hinders the ability to think clearly. Long-term stress has negative effects on the entire character of the dog, and its learning behaviour.

The meaning and significance of stress

Stress comprises a combination of pressure, strain, and tension. The term 'stress' was coined by the endocrinologist Hans Selye, who identified it as the cause of 'General Adaptation Syndrome.' A stress reaction is always produced by the joint actions of the nervous and endocrine systems.

It is necessary to distinguish positive stress, (eustress) – which drives us to achieve in activities that we like doing – from negative stress. In canine terms, these would be activities such as games or walks. The body demonstrates an optimum level of responsiveness and physical performance. Negative stress (distress) is something that really causes trouble for us humans, giving us the feeling of never being on top of everyday life. Indeed, intense or long-lasting stress can result in pathological changes in our body: the immune system is weakened; heart or cardiovascular problems may develop, or burnout syndrome and depressive episodes may occur. Chronic stress is one of the main causes of illness in our society.

Dogs experience stress in just the same way. Because of our cognitive abilities, humans are consciously aware of stress, and can possibly find ways to overcome it. Dogs can only fall back on their instinctive patterns of behaviour, and often react very quickly – and adversely – to stress.

They may, for example, scratch a great deal, bark more often, and, in the worst cases, self-harm (just as humans do). They can also begin to show avoidance behaviour, such as hiding or running away, and may even snap or bite.

New, unfamiliar situations or an extreme threat cause non-specific arousal in the brain; in this case, agitation or fear. If the situation does not calm down and the arousal level increases, activation of neural networks can trigger automatic behaviour to deal with a perceived potential emergency.

Stress hormones

Our dogs – just like us – are exposed to new situations on a daily basis, which generates stress hormones: chemical signalling substances that prompt certain biochemical reactions in the body.

Depending on the situation, different stress hormones are released: for example, fear leads to an increase in adrenaline; anger or rage the release of noradrenaline and testosterone (the male sex hormone).

Depression linked to loss of control and/or subordination leads to an increase in cortisol and a reduction in testosterone. All of these hormones are secreted in the adrenal gland and released into the bloodstream in acute situations.

After a brief period of tension (which, in normal circumstances, is essential to ensure that the animal can deal with whatever the situation demands), the body relaxes again, and physiological activity normalises once more. This process is described below, using the example of adrenaline.

Stress situation – fight or flight

Release of adrenaline – noradrenaline
Standard pattern of complete stress reaction
Acute alarm phase

The adrenal medulla releases the stress hormones adrenaline (flight hormone) and noradrenaline (fight hormone). Adrenaline is also created from noradrenaline by way of cortisol. Adrenaline facilitates a quick burst of energy, which is designed to allow the animal to flee from danger. The energy is supplied by the breakdown of body fat and release of glucose. Noradrenaline reduces sensitivity to pain by producing endorphins, the body's own feel-good hormones.

The effect of adrenaline on the animal
Heart rate increases (races). Blood pressure rises, stimulus conduction in the neural pathways is increased, and the threshold for neural stimuli is reduced. In addition, respiration quickens and lung capacity increases so that more air – and therefore more oxygen – can be absorbed. The gastro-intestinal tract and the bladder, on the other hand, cease their work. Other symptoms are sweating, dilated pupils, and dryness of the mucous membrane in the mouth.

The active phase
Using the energy that has been generated by the adrenaline.

The recovery phase
The symptoms subside. Circulation and metabolism return to normal. Arousal level in the neural system reduces. Hormone levels re-adjust. Duration: 3-6 minutes.

The incomplete stress reaction

If action is not taken to complete the process, the recovery phase will not occur, and arousal will continue. subjecting the heart and cardiovascular system to unnecessary pressure. The unused extra energy can actually cause illness: chronically raised adrenaline levels are linked to cardiac hypertrophy (enlarged heart).

Stress situation – loss of control
The release of cortisol

Cortisol is a hormone produced by the adrenal cortex; production increases under stress. In the short-term, this contributes to instigation of action by the animal; in the long-term, it can lead to mental and physical illness.

Cortisol has a greater range of effects than any other hormone, but, primarily, it is the metabolisation of carbohydrate, protein and fat, which results in the formation of glucose from the breakdown of muscle and fat tissue. Over the long-term, this gives rise to muscular atrophy and weakness, which, in turn, results in increased production and storage of fat, particularly around the abdominal and neck areas. Cortisol inhibits the immune system by reducing the production of antibodies (it has an immuno-suppressant effect), and also prevents the migration of leukocytes (white blood cells, which have a 'policing' function in the body) into an area of inflammation.

A rise in body temperature (fever), the normal reaction to an infection which renders germs harmless through this increase, is also inhibited. Wounds are also slower to heal, as the white blood cells cannot reach the affected areas.

In terms of its effects on the nerves, cortisol increases the brain's sensitivity to stimulation and reduces the seizure threshold. It can have both a euphoric and depressive affect on mood.

Cortisol is crucial in overcoming extremely stressful situations, but if it is continuously released into the system, so that the body is in a permanent state of stress, it has very harmful effects as the body never returns to a normal state, and new stressors constantly add to the level of arousal.

Very simply presented, the foregoing are the biochemical reasons why a body absolutely must have recovery phases in order to stay physically and mentally healthy. This is particularly important during growth, as studies suggest that young animals and humans who experience a large amount of stress at an early stage are more sensitive to stress later in life than animals and people who have grown up in a relaxed environment. (Source: *Stress: It's Worse Than You Think* in *Psychology Today*. 2006)

Dr Ursula Zimmermann

Stress in dogs can occur as a result of being under- or over-challenged, harsh or incorrect training, excessive stimulation, the incorrect interpretation of canine communication, lack of attachment to a human, and traumatic experiences. A sudden outbreak of inappropriate behaviour because of excessive stress can overtake any dog, regardless of how well socialised she is. Dogs send us signals when they are feeling uncomfortable and suffering from stress, and, as with any creature, their levels of stress depend on the background and constitution of the individual.

A puppy who has early, positive experience of many stimuli from the outside world will not go through as much stress at a later stage as one that has grown up in a very isolated environment.

There are certainly some basic structures in canine communication, but every dog is an individual with her own way of expressing herself. Much has been written on the subject of calming signals and stress signals (scratching and yawning), but such signals should always be understood in context and not taken as stand-alone communications. I find some of these interpretations very exaggerated; for example, not every episode of scratching is a stress signal, and often my dogs just enjoy a good yawn – without being the slightest bit stressed.

Every dog owner should take a good look at his ways of expressing himself, as these impact on his dog every day – whether the behaviour is conscious or unconscious – and can confuse the dog and cause him stress.

It is important to learn to observe your dog closely and understand him. The more you pay attention to your dog's methods of expressing himself, the better you will be at interpreting and understanding his behaviour.

Examples of what may cause stress in a dog
- Travelling (especially air travel)
- Separation anxiety
- Children or contact with certain people
- Noises and unfamiliar situations
- General anxieties
- Change of owner
- Moving to a new home

Just enjoying a good yawn ...

- Holiday and/or a stay in kennels
- Boredom/lack of stimulation
- Over-challenged
- Lack of socialisation with other dogs and the wider environment
- A training method that is too harsh and insensitive
- 'Ball junkie' – when dogs become too fixated on objects
- Too little rest time
- Excessive attention from a human
- Limited opportunity to retreat to their own space
- Too much or too little contact with humans
- Isolation/kept in a kennel
- Several dogs in the same household
- Bullying in puppy walking groups or in parks
- Negative experiences with other dogs (biting incidents)

- Punishment
- Being deliberately ignored for a long time
- Death of the owner
- Overworked (service dogs – rescue dogs, guide dogs for the blind, therapy dogs – who are not given any opportunity to relax)
- Being used as a substitute partner
- Misinterpretation of communication:
  - between dog and dog
  - between dog and human
  - between human and dog
- Disregarding the signals the dog sends us

Examples of stress symptoms in dogs

- Constant/excessive barking
- Agitated or hyperactive behaviour
- Allergies, skin problems
- Scratching and constant licking of the skin until it is raw
- Trembling
- Nervous and/or aggressive behaviour

Elsa, the Irish Wolfhound
puppy, relaxing.

- Constant display of calming signals (lip licking)
- Constant panting
- Soiling (urine and faeces)
- Regular vomiting
- Lack of concentration
- Unwillingness to engage in training
- Lead aggression; biting other dogs when on the lead
- Constantly yapping and biting own lead
- Not wanting to tolerate any closeness or touch
- Wanting to chase everything and jump up at people
- Constant drinking
- Fearfulness
- Constant mounting

Continuous music/noise during the dog's rest periods should be avoided, as this can also be a big stress factor.

A relaxed walk in the
woods.

Dog Relax

All of these examples of stress symptoms should be viewed in context: when and how often does the symptom occur? In what situation does the behaviour become evident, and what was the trigger? Has the dog perhaps had previous negative experiences in this particular area?

The more intensively you involve yourself with canine communication and body language, the more sensitive you will be to recognising and interpreting your dog's stress signals. In this way, stressful situations can even be avoided, or your dog can be reconditioned to deal with these previously stressful situations.

A trusting, free from fear relationship between human and dog will result in her gladly forming an attachment to you. But remember, if you work with dogs, you also have to work on yourself.

Last but not least: even children these days are sometimes over-scheduled from one end of the week to the other. It's the same for dogs; either the owners are so apathetic that they don't do any work at all with their dogs, or the dogs are fully booked all week doing agility, man-trailing, dog dancing, and meeting other canines at the park, which is completely over the top and likely to cause stress. Each of these activities is good, but in moderation. Your dog will still love you even if you simply take her for a sniff around in the woods and fields, enjoying time and nature together.

GREAT THINGS COME IN SMALL PACKAGES – THE SIGNIFICANCE OF COMMUNICATION AND BODY LANGUAGE

Dog language

Every dog owner should respect and appreciate her dog, and give him the opportunity to understand us. He speaks dog language and we speak human language – how is he supposed to know what we are telling him?

Very often I have seen dogs being talked at; entire essays and instruction manuals. When this happens, the dog will react by becoming irritated and confused, the constant barrage of sound rendering him incapable of taking in any information at all as he has simply become inured to the stream of words. The same is true for us, if we have the radio on all the time in the background, for instance. If we actually concentrate on what is being broadcast, we take in what we hear, otherwise, we register noise coming from the radio, but don't really take it in. And sometimes we just block it out totally.

Many people expect dogs to understand them straight away, and may even become annoyed when the dog doesn't follow a prompt. An analogy: if you're travelling in a foreign country, you don't understand immediately what the locals say to you, do you? Foreign languages have to be learnt. I once went on a trip from the Canary Islands to Marrakesh in Morocco, and felt at a complete loss because I didn't understand the language there; even the sign language really confused me. So why do we expect dogs to understand everything immediately when we ourselves can't ...?

Successful communication is when the sender imparts something that the receiver can absorb and implement. In general, the message sent matches the message received, and we can say that understanding (communication) has taken place. However, in understanding between human and dog, very great difficulties often occur, so that the sender's message is not understood by the receiver. Learn to 'read' your dog so that you can understand her messages. We humans pay too little attention to the non-verbal communications from dogs; I know this from my own experience. Going back to basics and learning to 'read' your dog requires much motivation, discipline, and high levels of awareness and alertness. But it's worth all the effort! Every change begins with one small step – start now!

Dogs express themselves clearly, although sometimes very subtly. If you have opened your mind to an awareness of your dog, then you will not miss the signals. You can discover a great deal about your dog, simply by studying her facial expressions, as facial muscles are closely connected with the brain's emotional centre.

Humans and dogs *can* communicate with each other, but some of the ways they express themselves are very different.

Approaching each other
Humans approach each other directly; dogs, on the other hand, never approach head-on, but from the side, thereby avoiding direct eye contact.

Eye contact
In conversation, people generally look directly at each other, making eye contact, showing that they are interested in what is being said.

A dog, however, finds this intimidating, and may feel threatened, as constant, unwavering eye contact amongst dogs in a group is used to threaten and establish dominance. Conversely, an averted face upsets a dog as much as it does a baby (a baby will also dislike being shown a profile or three-quarter profile).

The greeting ritual
Humans sometimes greet each other warmly with physical contact; a handshake, hug, or kiss. A person would find it natural to want to cuddle or hug his dog, but, to the dog, this kind of physical contact is often used by other dogs to restrict and control each other.

Bear in mind that some dogs will feel threatened by direct eye contact for any length of time with anyone, regardless of who it is, and if they are stroked too enthusiastically.

As I have noticed in my work with my therapy animals, dogs can differentiate between 'dog language' and 'human language' once they have learnt to understand two communication systems. My dogs have learnt not to feel intimidated when someone stands or steps over them, or hugs them. Dogs who have not learnt this, or who have had traumatic experiences in this context, will undoubtedly have problems with this for some time. Proceed with extreme caution, particularly if the two of you have not yet established a trusting relationship. We have so many expectations of our family pets, but very often forget that some human behaviour can create confusion and cause stress to our animals.

I advise every dog owner to learn about canine communication and the dog's means of expression, and maybe even take a course. Film analysis is very helpful in this respect, as you can watch the sequences in slow motion, enabling you to see the very subtle but very important nuances of canine communication, although this will sometimes mean viewing the film several times before you identify these.

When I am out walking or at the park, I am always meeting people who react very

There is clear communication within a dog pack.

unsympathetically when I look after the welfare of my dog by – for example – stepping in to sort out a game that has turned into something that is no fun at all. What started out as a friendly game has become a threatening and oppressive situation, although other dog owners may say "Oh, they are having such a lovely game!" It is equally wrong to imagine that dogs can sort out everything on their own; this may well be the case in a group of dogs that are always together, but when dogs meet in parks or on walks, it is always more or less at random.

Learn to detect and understand your dog's language: it will make many things easier and help you to identify your dog's wishes and needs much more easily. Also, become aware of the way that you express yourself, as much of our body language – to which your dog is exposed on a daily basis – can confuse her. Each of our physical movements makes a strong statement, and has a huge effect on a dog's behaviour and mental state, particularly so when the relationship between dog and human is not based on trust and love.

Check that you are really expressing yourself clearly, as speech, expression and body language can sometimes be ambiguous. Dogs express themselves in clearly defined ways; humans sometimes do not, which is what confuses a dog. I will address this further in the next chapter.

Less is more

Thankfully, research has now disproved the old chestnut about the aggressive alpha wolf pack leader. Alpha wolves do not always achieve their pack position by fighting alone. They act as advocate; responsible for representing the interests of the pack. The alpha wolf leads his pack by expressing himself clearly and with an air of authority.

"What humans should learn from experienced wolf parents is how to achieve social predictability, how to maintain an air of authority, even in stressful situations, and how to occupy a brief leadership role and make decisions in a quiet and relaxed manner." – Günther Bloch, author, 2007

This is exactly why dogs often simply don't take seriously angry, screaming people – and don't understand them, either. If a human acts out of emotion, he is no longer 'master of the situation,' which causes a dog to feel very uncertain, as the qualities of the alpha wolf – calm, clarity and an air of authority – are not present.

This is why it is pointless to attempt training when you are angry or upset. Happy motivation in an angry atmosphere is just not possible, and you will only succeed in making your dog feel stressed.

If you find this happening during a training session, simply either stop the session and just walk quietly for a while (walking can help clear your head), or do some breathing and relaxation exercises to centre yourself and regain your composure. Dogs do not understand when they are shouted at, or threatened with punishment (which should not be necessary in any case, as positive reinforcement is a much better and more productive way of training). Never vent your pent-up emotions on a dog or any animal. In any case, there's no point trying to train a dog when you are angry, as she will sense your emotion and react to it negatively.

As dog owners, we learn to treat our dog with respect. If your emotions sometimes threaten to boil over despite your best efforts, don't be too hard on yourself; you're on the right track to

You can achieve a great deal with just visual cues.

DOG RELAX

DOGS MIRROR OUR EMOTIONS

How do we deal with this?	
↓	↓
We ignore it	We perceive the emotions and change them
↓	↓
Stress	We become relaxed

developing a new awareness of your dog's needs, which is fantastic. The more sensitive we are when dealing with dogs, the more we can refine our body language: large, crude gestures can be scaled back to clear but subtle signals.

For instance, in the case of the visual cue for the 'sit' command, at the beginning it's often necessary to very obviously lift the whole arm, but in time you will need only raise your finger. The few spoken commands that you do use will be clear and unambiguous, because, in this instance, less really is more, and these finely-tuned signals will be clearly understood by the receiver.

Remember that our sensitive canine friends react to our smallest movements, and know the exact state of our mood. Sometimes it seems as if we communicate to our dogs far more of our inner selves than we realise: unfortunately, this means that dogs also detect our weak points and sometimes exploit these ...

Dog Zen

I can well remember times when I waited for my dog (or dogs), quietly fuming with anger, at the edge of a field, because, once again, they had the scent of a rabbit and were chasing after it. In my mind, I sometimes pictured how I would teach them a lesson. I was beside myself and caught up in my emotions. But what use was that? None at all!

Of course, it's not ideal when one of my dogs does an arbitrary sprint across a field, but I have three hounds with very strong hunting instincts, and, in spite of being well-trained and generally obedient, sometimes their genetic programming gets the better of them and they do what they have been bred to do: act independently.

These days, if one of my dogs takes off like this without permission and I start to feel angry, I take a couple of deep breaths, quietly and deliberately breathing deeply from the stomach and not the chest. I remind myself that my dogs are not deliberately annoying me but simply following their instincts. I focus on something in my surroundings and concentrate on being aware of all the beautiful things around me. Together with the breathing exercise, I find this very helpful in achieving a more relaxed state. Now, if my dog comes back after a short time and is happy, I can share his joy; when my Podenco comes running towards me, he radiates joie-de-vivre. My new attitude has produced many changes for the better in my relationship with my dogs.

It is obviously important to set boundaries, as these will give a feeling of security, just as with children. Bear in mind that within large dog packs or in a wolf pack, positive reinforcement is not the only disciplinary method used, although within the human/dog relationship, there's no reason at all why it can't be used in isolation. Punishment should never mean directing physical violence towards a dog, or any animal.

Luckily, all my dogs disappear for a short run and come back almost immediately.

Dog Zen method

Living and behaving with relaxed awareness is an objective in which many people invest a lot of time and money, in an effort to achieve this 'magic' state.

Dogs provide us with a wonderful challenge: to clarify our emotional state in order to grow and develop a new potential and love of life. Dogs continually stretch us in this respect by mirroring our weaknesses and deficiencies, our impatience, anger and rage, and lack of clarity.

I have been consulted by some owners whose animals have suddenly begun exhibiting problematic behaviour. It may be that dogs belonging to very insecure, possibly nervous owners, who give them free rein to do whatever they like, may suddenly become confrontational and bark at everything around them. Moods and emotions are transferred to the dog via the lead like some form of energy, and the dogs sense that there's not a strong, authoritative personality at the other end. Uncertainty or anxiety is communicated to the dog in this way, and she also becomes nervous. To disguise this (no dog likes to appear frail or weak), she may adopt an aggressive, over-confident attitude.

DOG RELAX

"Man cannot not communicate"
– P Watzlawick psychologist and philosopher, 1969

This basic precept tells us very clearly that all behaviour and every movement imparts a message, and even when we don't say a word, our body continues to 'talk' – sometimes it seems as if a look or a gesture can express more than words ever could.

At the beginning of my training courses, I teach participants to be aware of their posture, approach and emotional state, and to be relaxed in their breathing. A bad or tense attitude will send the dog correspondingly negative signals. If we are not breathing freely, we appear uptight, with contracted chest, often exacerbated by tense, hunched shoulders, a sort of protective reflex when we are anxious or worried. When tension builds up in one part of the body, various other parts are also affected. For this reason, I find it is very important to become aware of our breathing, as this

can bring about positive change. Deep and relaxed breathing enables more oxygen to flow into our lungs and we can think more efficiently.

Freeing our breathing brings us new energy, and liberates us from tension, as well as helping us stand straighter and centre ourselves. Many of the relaxation techniques originating in Asia focus on developing relaxed breathing.

Sometimes, people unconsciously assume a posture that expresses extreme tension, and sometimes the complete opposite as their muscle tone seems totally de-energised and slack, making it appear that the individual has absolutely no life force or joie de vivre. At both ends of this spectrum, bad posture can not only block energy flow in the body, but also affect our emotions. If you're a bit sceptical about this, try the following exercises, one after the other:

A) Stand up and then hunch your shoulders and hang your head (feel free to exaggerate). Breathe in a few times. Walk around the room a few times. Observe how you are feeling.

B) Then stand up very straight. Imagine you are a king or queen, proud and elegant. Move around the room whilst maintaining a posture that is very straight and tall but also relaxed.

Can you feel the difference?

Walking tall and moving freely signals a kind of looseness and relaxation in the context of normal body tension (a certain amount of tension is essential in order to live, of course).

As already stated, dogs react to the signals that we give out. Sometimes, for no obvious reason, a dog may suddenly engage in unusual behaviour, but this could be directly linked to us. (Of course, there are also many other reasons why a dog may do this.) In this instance, sometimes it's enough

DOG RELAX

No communication: "together, but alone ..."

... and active communication.

that we change something about our attitude and/or posture, whereupon, the dog's behaviour may return to normal. So, just as an erect posture and looking up rather than down has a bearing on our manner, our 'internal and external presence' can be used to communicate a sense of reassurance to our dog. This is also an important aspect of non-verbal communication.

One example of this I remember very well. On a training course, I got to know a woman with a young sheepdog. During the sessions, they made a great team, but, on the day of the test, the woman was so nervous that her agitation and doubts were communicated to the dog via the lead. When it was their turn for the test, the dog just did his own thing: he pulled on the lead instead of walking to heel, and then began to bite the lead and clown around. The dog could sense his mistress' uncertainty and her weaknesses, and was apparently taking advantage of them. After several re-runs and some instruction from the examiner, the situation changed for the better. However, during the test the woman was not fulfilling her leadership role, which she had done previously in training, and so did not pass the test.

This is a very obvious example of how important it is that a handler communicates clearly and decisively with a dog. The importance of clear communication is obvious because it is the prerequisite to many leadership roles, and is intensively taught (eg managerial training).

We can never deceive a dog, as she knows exactly what we are thinking and feeling. It's easier, however, to deceive humans. Many people smile and say they are fine, when, in reality, they're not; it seems we are compelled to maintain a façade. Insensitive people are easiest to deceive as those who are receptive to communicating with awareness will be more sensitive to others' emotional signals.

These days, there is less and less direct communication between people, and when we do talk to each other, we are often at cross-purposes. Less time is spent really relaxing, and we are prepared to invest only limited amounts of time in what we do.

In the book *The Little Prince* by Saint-Exupery, a fox and the Little Prince meet. The fox looks at the Little Prince for a long time in silence. "Please ... tame me!" he says. "I would like to," says the Little Prince, "but I haven't got much time. I have to find some friends and learn many things." "You only know the things that you tame." replies the fox. "People have no time any more to get to know something. They buy everything ready-made from the shops. But as there are no shops where you can buy friends, people have no friends any more. If you want a friend, tame me!"

Then, a few lines further on: "Taming means getting familiar with one another, but humans don't have time for this any more." Relating this to our dogs, not enough time is taken in getting to know our animals. Life is busier now, yes, but a dog needs a lot of time and attention.

It is very important that there is communication between human and dog. I so often see people out for a walk with their dog: they may be wearing headphones, or are on the phone, or writing a text message whilst the dog runs ahead or shambles along behind. Seeing these scenes often leaves me with the impression of a pair that are 'together but alone;' walking together, but each in their own world.

Dogs have a pronounced willingness to communicate, but if their efforts are not acknowledged, ie they get no response or reaction, then the urge to communicate withers and dies, as the dog, understandably, becomes fed-up when it seems as if none of the signals that he sends to the human arrives. Many dog owners don't even notice when their dog makes eye contact with them. If this communication is lost, a large amount of effort is required to revive it. Let your dog know that you recognise his approach and respond to it appropriately. Dark glasses do not allow good communication, and can confuse your signals (see photos on page 34).

"Human language serves to express, feign or hide feelings. A lie is an impossibility in canine language." – unknown

Dogs have their own language and rules comprising very unambiguous body language with few sounds. This body language is what enables dogs to learn how to get close to one another.

Dogs have very acute powers of observation; they react to every physical gesture and expression, no matter how small, and really do notice every nuance of our expressions and emotions.

Wearing sunglasses means that the dog is looking at an anonymous' face: he appears perplexed ...

... but as soon as he can see a face properly, he can begin to communicate.

They are scanning us constantly, one objective being to scrutinise their human social partner intensely on a daily basis. It is because dogs are so good at assessing us that they are used intensively in animal-assisted therapy.

So, if we call our dog to us when we are angry, despite using a pleasant tone, she will sense from our body language and smell how we are really feeling (and is why she will come very grudgingly and submissively). So, if our verbal and non-verbal expressions don't match, the dog will recognise this inconsistency – two signals that do not fit together: our anger and the pleasant – although feigned – tone of voice – and become confused and stressed.

We can recognise the problems that our mixed messages cause our companions and work on avoiding this, making communication between us more clear-cut and less ambiguous.

Even a tiny change in our posture produces an immediate reaction from the dog. As shown in the photos below, a stooped posture is perceived as threatening, whilst an erect posture elicits positive interest from the dog.

Dogs link certain words with an action. This is generally achieved by means of classical conditioning; ie they learn the meaning of the word (and/or what they are supposed to do) by being rewarded for the desired behaviour. For example, a dog – we will call him Bertie – has learnt:

Command	Required response
Come	I am supposed to come
Here	I have to come and sit down
Off	I am not allowed there

People who talk a lot with their dog sometimes use phrases such as these when they are annoyed and want to get their dog out of the flowerbed.

"Get off there."
"Here, off there now."
"Come, here, off!"

Eh? What is the dog supposed to do? Come (come), (here) sit down, off (get off).

We've all used these kinds of mixed messages from time to time; monitor yourself and see when you next do it!

One of my dogs is used in children's therapy to help with concentration training. It's fascinating to watch what happens, for instance, when a child gives the visual cue for 'sit' but actually says 'down.' After a short pause for thought, my dog almost always decides to go with the visual cue, suggesting

Two different postures: leaning forward with wide open eyes causes the dog to feel threatened and react immediately with the appropriate calming signals; an upright posture and friendly gaze result in the dog reacting with a friendly, eager attitude.

that his perception is more tuned to body language than verbal commands.

Three examples of this:

- A woman was training her young Hovawart crossbreed. As the dog was in his adolescent phase, the woman needed to be firmer and more deliberate in the way she dealt with him, and to give him the 'down' command really loudly. Because the dog sensed the woman's uncertainty, he quite obviously messed about and kept standing up from the down position as soon as the woman turned her back on him. The dog trainer advised the woman to speak more loudly. She admitted that speaking loudly and shouting was a problem for her. She then made another attempt at the exercise. She approached her dog (her gait was not very purposeful, more like a casual dawdle, which meant that the dog stood up again, wagging his tail and happily waiting for his mistress). With a smile, the woman then tried to shout 'down.' The dog, sensing the ambivalence between her body language, voice and actual intention, simply looked at her, waiting to see what game came next. This situation was so clear-cut I would have liked to have filmed it.

When the dog trainer repeated the exercise and approached the dog with an authoritative posture, appropriate expression, and deliberate gait, the dog did not wag his tail: he was very attentive. When the trainer gave an assertive 'down' command, the dog responded immediately, and then stayed where he should.

This clearly shows the importance of our posture, expression and voice in dog training. When we have problems expressing ourselves clearly, the dog won't (want to) understand us ...

- A dog owner who was rather insecure in the handling of his rescued retriever, and who wanted to protect him all the time, was having big problems with his four-legged friend because he gave too many commands at once. The retriever had taken to picking up stones and chewing them, which had potentially calamitous repercussions for his teeth. When this happened, his owner stood limply in front of the dog and gave a continuous stream of commands: "Out," "No," "Leave that," "You'll break your teeth on that!"etc. Understandably, the dog just carried on chewing the stone ... The owner then placed his hand near the dog's muzzle, hoping to prompt the dog to give him the stone, and gave the commands again. The dog turned his head away, unimpressed, drew back his lips to issue a quick warning, and then carried on chewing. It became very clear that the dog didn't take his owner seriously at all.

I am convinced that if the owner had stood up straight and said "Out" or "No" loudly and deliberately, and confidently taken hold of the dog's muzzle, the animal would have taken the request seriously and given up the stone.

● An elderly man who had recently had a hip operation, and whose Rottweiler had died, got himself a young Border Collie. The man was in despair about his dog's behaviour (he barked constantly and was uncontrollable), and so contacted a dog training school for help. In the case of this human/dog pairing, it was noticeable that the man's restricted mobility meant that he couldn't physically keep up with the dog. He tried to compensate for this by using a very authoritarian style of communication. The dog gave the impression of being completely under-stimulated and stressed.

I noted that the dog was very motivated to do everything right, but was so excited that he barked all the time, so that, even when he carried out a command correctly, his lead was immediately tugged to tell him to stop barking. I hardly ever heard his owner give any praise, but on the few occasions that he did say something positive, his tone was such that the dog could never have understood it as praise. I had the feeling that the dog was simply lacking confirmation of the things that he had done right, and wasn't being praised: barking was simply his way of trying to attract some attention and acknowledgement from his owner. (Of course, there was the additional complication that this man had chosen the one breed of dog that was probably the most unsuitable for him, given his age and state of health.)

I could cite so many more examples, but the basic problem is always the same: the conflict between body language, facial expression, and what is actually said. If owners expressed themselves more clearly, the lives of many dogs would be a great deal easier.

A dog, on the other hand, is always present in everything that he is thinking and feeling at that moment. He cannot pretend, and, in contrast to humans, is always sincere and genuine in everything he expresses and everything he does. When he is happy, he shows it. A really happy dog (the emphasis here is on 'really,' as, unfortunately, tail-wagging can also be a sign of agitation, as well as happiness) will never deceive you and bite for no reason.

By the same token, an agitated dog who has given notice that he is about to attack, will not suddenly become happy.

And as a reminder ...
In time, you will become more and more aware of the overall impression that you give your dog, including your (good) posture, expression, and gestures. Your dog will notice your new cohesive approach, but will also immediately note any ambivalence. For instance, if you want to praise

your dog, but are really annoyed or under stress at that point and expressing this through a tense posture, your dog will probably be unable to understand the praise, and may receive it as something negative. At that point, you will appear insincere to him.

A dog is always sincere in his emotions and how he expresses them – and you must be the same.

UNITED WE STAND: THE HUMAN/DOG TEAM

"Attachment constitutes firstly the phenomenon that an animal (in this case the dog) forms a close social relationship with another individual." – Karl E Zimen, author, 1992

Authors H Weidt and D Berlowitz, who defined the attachment theory, apply it to the human/dog relationship and describe it as follows: "That invisible bond, which we also call attachment, can be formed between two unequal partners."

Author Dr Dorit Feddersen-Petersen describes the harmonious relationship between dogs, as well as between the dog and his human social partner, by characterising mainly socially positive behaviour, such as contact and play behaviour, as having a special quality which can be labelled as attachment.

I believe that an attachment based on trust in the human/dog team is very important. However, by attachment I do not mean that a dog always walks perfectly to heel, never lets his owner out of his sight for a second, and maintains constant eye contact. This kind of behaviour is often considered the sign of a good relationship, but it's simply acquired behaviour which is well received in dog obedience tests, and is often combined with intense levels of authority.

There is a big difference between training and attachment!

In the same way, attachment means much more than 'attaching' the dog to you with treats and constant attention. Giving treats elicits short-term attentiveness at most, but no real attachment.

To illustrate my view on human/dog attachment, I use the explanatory model for yoga. These days, yoga is generally accepted everywhere, and is used as a relaxation technique by everyone from business managers to housewives. The word 'yoga' comes from 'yuig,' and means something like 'attach' or 'join together' – in the sense of bringing the spirit into harmony with the body – forming an attachment in order to maintain good health.

The bond is the basis for all else
I respect my dog and would like to be his pack leader, so that he will trust me totally and I will try not to disappoint him. The security of this arrangement enables him to attach himself to me with complete confidence, and engage with the world around him in positive terms.

For wolves, who live within a social framework, it is very important that there is an alpha male/pack leader, or leading couple. Dogs live in similar social structures; if they cannot find direction in the pack leader, they have to assume this position themselves, and bear the full weight of responsibility of sorting out everything, and protecting their 'pack' (their owner). With some dogs, this can mean that they become very aggressive, and will vigorously defend all their resources in order, of course, to protect their pack (human), causing the dogs much stress in the process.

Examples of a lack of authority and leadership
I know a very powerful Golden Retriever, who has always been treated like a little lapdog. He never really had any proper training with rules, and, when still a puppy, was considered a little sweetie; later becoming the sweet 'fat boy.' In the absence of any guidance or boundaries, the dog inevitably assumed the leadership position, and these days it is he who shows his owners where he wants to walk, for example. If he decides to walk faster or run, his owner is dragged along behind, going at his pace. He barks at all other dogs as soon as he sees them. His owners don't have any authority, and can't always control him, which has already led to some very difficult situations.

On a training course, I met a very gentle, small woman who had a heavyweight Staffy cross (I am not prejudiced toward these dogs, as they have a very strong character with a high tolerance threshold. It is, however, unfortunate when these dogs fall into the wrong hands ...). The woman seemed very unsure, even nervous, and had a very cautious manner. This dog was also extremely spoilt, and had not received any training appropriate to his temperament. "He used to be so sweet and cuddly," his owner said. When he reached adolescence, the woman had great problems as the dog began to behave very oddly towards humans and animals, snarling at everything and everyone. In fact, he was just trying to fulfil his role as leader and protect and defend his insecure owner. It was also very clear in this case that the dog had assumed the position of boss.

"Pack leaders (including humans) have – in addition to their generally acknowledged rights – numerous obligations. Apart from demonstrating a certain coolness,' which is very impressive to inexperienced members of the pack/group, they have to take their social responsibility seriously."
– Günther Bloch, author, 2007

As a dog owner, you should be committed to assuming the position of leader, but this does not mean that you must become domineering or harsh in your relationship with your dog: authority is not inevitably linked with violence.

"Authority in the broadest sense is a social position allocated to an institution or person, and which leads to other people following them in their thinking and actions." – Wikipedia

A good pack leader is distinguished by clarity, firmness, reliability, strength, and self-confidence. An alpha wolf is never conspicuously aggressive or loud, he is simply self-confident with an air of authority.

"What humans should learn from experienced wolf parents is how to achieve social predictability, how to maintain an air of authority, even in stressful situations, and how to occupy a brief leadership role and make decisions in a quiet and relaxed manner." – Günther Bloch, author, 2007

When my Podenco follows his instincts and races across a field, it doesn't mean that we have no attachment to each other, or that the attachment is a negative one. Our attachment is not

DOG RELAX

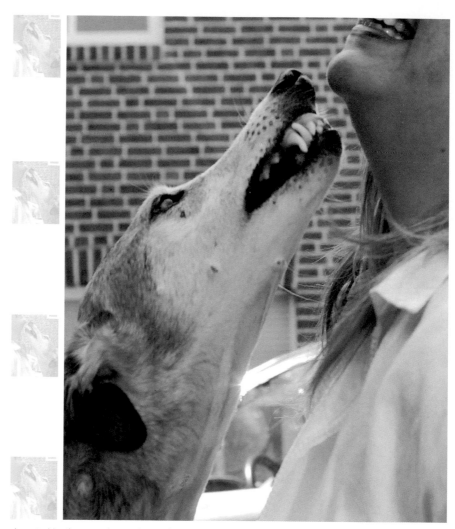

disrupted by this unauthorised sprint (it is not desirable from my point of view, but, in terms of the Podenco's behavioural repertoire, it has been selectively bred for this over many years), but at that moment the dog has simply followed his instincts.

I have noticed that the mental work and the massages I have done with my dogs has made our attachment much more intense. The dogs are noticeably more attentive, and always keep an eye on me, though none of them is the kind of dog that is always at their owner's heels. That kind of dependence would be stressful for both dog and owner, although when I am working as a coach, I see this kind of behaviour very often, and usually find that the dogs have never been trained or taught about boundaries.

One should not, however, try to generalise attachment. I have often seen 'attachment tests' in magazines for human and dog, the answers to which are supposed to determine the intensity of attachment between them. However, every dog breed – and even every dog – has a different type of attachment relationship with a human. As I have already mentioned, Podencos are bred to behave very naturally and independently; in contrast, the Pug generally trots along in a well-behaved manner next to or behind his owner, though this does not necessarily mean that the Pug's attachment to his human is more intense than the Poenco's.

Dog training requires
- rules, boundaries
- discipline
- structure, clarity
- consistency
- enjoyment

– all combined with our love and respect.

Some people, as soon as they hear the words 'boundaries, discipline, consistency,' are worried their dog will think that they do not love her any more if they attempt to teach these regimes, but in this belief they are confusing human and canine feelings. Have you ever seen how mother wolves deal with their cubs? Or have you perhaps observed puppies and how they interact with one another? They are not always gentle: wolf and dog parents are strict, clear and consistent, but they still love their offspring. There are obvious structures within the pack, and, in some matters, the pack leader tolerates no nonsense whatsoever from the youngsters. Despite this, all of the dogs like to be around him and want to lie near him. Similarly, humans who deliberately train with structure, clarity, discipline, consistency, and love are respected and liked very much by their dogs.

In contrast, dogs who lack this structure metaphorically walk all over their human. Often, these are the small dogs, who have been bred to look a bit like babies (big eyes and high forehead). With such a small and sweet-looking creature, training sometimes falls by the wayside. A small, yappy dog is still considered 'sweet,' whereas a large dog that barks is 'ferocious' or a 'fighting' dog, but this is exactly the same aberrant behaviour, simply displayed by different types of dog.

It is particularly upsetting to see little dogs pulling on the lead, in the process, building a huge amount of tension in their necks.

We humans are in search of perfection and growth: but our dogs? We must really try to satisfy their needs (mental stimulation, sufficient exercise, time and attention) – or else they are obliged to live alongside us and slowly lose their canine identity.

There's one more very important element to dog training: laughter and play. Have a go at simply playing with your dog; rediscover your childish sense of joy in play, and learn to actively enjoy your dog.

Incidentally, laughter is a great help in reducing stress hormones levels and releasing pleasure hormones, as adrenaline and cortisol levels reduce and pleasure hormone (endorphins) levels increase

when you laugh, which quickly relaxes you. The healing power of laughter is considered ever more important by researchers. Gelotology (laughing and laughter) studies have demonstrated that laughing can even relieve pain through the release of anti-inflammatory substances. Laughing also strengthens the cardio-vascular system.

Have you laughed yet today?

"A day without a laugh is a wasted day." – Charlie Chaplin, actor

The most recent trials carried out by Dorit Feddersen-Petersen show that dogs are also certainly able to laugh, although it remains to be proved whether this also releases endorphins.

Keeping your cool: impulse control

An impulse is always a reaction to a stimulus. A dog's senses and nerve cells respond to an external event or from within the dog, and call up a reaction by means of electrical signals from the brainstem.

In humans, we describe impulse control as self-control, whereas in animals it is reaction control. Young dogs like to run up to other dogs the minute they see them; very agitated dogs also have problems with self-control. It is important for her later life that the young dog learns to control her reaction (I see a dog, I run over to it). If impulse control is omitted from the young dog's training, she will continue to try and run up to other dogs. Impulse control is learnt gradually, and not completedly mastered until the dog becomes adult, because, in young dogs, the neuro-biological structures are not yet mature, although they are present. Exercises in impulse control training are actually enormously important for all dogs.

Impulse control, however, does not mean carrying out commands such as 'sit, down, heel,' as should be evident by now.

Many people burden their animal by exposing him to an enormous number of stimuli (overstimulation). As already described in the section on stress, dogs are today exposed to very many different activities, sometimes even on a daily basis. All of these well-intentioned opportunities for action and the constant exercise they entail can, however, be too much, as the dog simply cannot process them all. The state of excitement (signals from the brainstem) is constantly high, and, as a result, the dog may be labelled hyperactive and a 'problem dog,' when, in fact, it's just that he doesn't – perhaps can't – get any peace.

Dog Relax is a very good solution under these circumstances, for both dog and owner. Tactile stimulation will help calm restless dogs as the animal becomes more relaxed, and the hormone oxytocin is released into the body (there's a more detailed explanation of this in the section *What massage does*).

It is important to remember that a 'manageable' dog is not necessarily a relaxed dog, as this requires the absence of any physical tension. Dogs are also able to relax by themselves, using their initiative to assume the 'down' position so that muscle tone relaxes. Maintaining the 'sit' position, however, necessitates a certain degree of muscle tension. In some obedience tests, the dog is not allowed to lie down when he wants to, resulting in a clash of impulses which can cause confusion and stress. The body wants to relax, the dog wants to lie down in order to allow it, but the obedience test demands that he stay in the 'sit' position, which means that his muscles remain tensed.

If you would now like to begin practising relaxation with your dog, use treats only in the initial

Amigo has learnt to sit-stay on command, and is doing it, even though his favourite toy is temptingly flying through the air.

An example of how dogs learn

Every dog learns in a different way. Learning entails the opportunity to understand (the absorption of information), to make connections, to internalise (creation and storage of memories), and to remember (retrievability of information). Every training session should be built up slowly and patiently, otherwise dogs become overstretched (stress again), and lose their enjoyment of learning.

Learning begins with the imitation of that which the pups see their mother doing. Later on, dogs also like to copy things done by others of their species, both good and bad. If – as already explained – a dog is constantly talked at, at some point he will become 'deaf' to the noise (and will become 'deaf' in any case if there are no consequences for him when he doesn't carry out commands). In behavioural biology, this is called habituation: if stimuli occur at an early stage without there being any consequences for the dog, a process in the nervous system means that the reaction to it becomes weaker, or even ceases altogether.

Pavlov's classical conditioning is very well known in relation to dog training, as is operant conditioning (based on research by psychologist B F Skinner), whilst both systems are meshed for use in trick training, for example. Operant – or instrumental – conditioning uses positive and negative reinforcement. Operant conditioning focuses primarily on spontaneous behaviour for specific purposes. This method is also known as 'learning through success,' which means it is very important to reward the dog immediately after the activity – within 1-2 seconds. If the reward is delayed or there is none, over the long-term, what the dog has learnt will be forgotten.

Dog Relax

Lying down like this is relaxing for a dog.

stages on the relaxation mat because tasty treats can increase your dog's level of excitement. In any case, the dog is not supposed to relax in order that he receives a treat!

A summary of Dog Relax

Dog Relax training is not intended to replace 'normal' training, but focuses instead on achieving and maintaining health and relaxation for both human and dog.

The human has to learn to stay relaxed around his dog, even in stressful situations, in order not to transmit unnecessary stress to the dog. A relaxed person expresses himself much more clearly and intelligibly, and will also feel better in himself.

This different approach to training deepens the attachment between human and dog. As the human's perception becomes more intensive and aware, he learns more about how to communicate with his dog. The dog experiences training and obedience on a new basis, and is motivated to respond. At the same time, however, the dog is also learning to switch from the enjoyment of movement to relaxation, which helps with impulse control training in everyday life.

Stress levels in dogs can be reduced through touch and massage, and they will soon feel and appreciate the benefits. This method also helps preserve good health because, for example, a relaxed dog will develop fewer internal blockages because of tense musculature. This benefit is of great importance for dogs who suffer from severe anxiety, or who, perhaps, have been mistreated.

DOG RELAX – WHAT IT DOES
* The human-dog/attachment is nurtured and deepened
* The approach promotes communication
* A new basis for training and obedience is created
* Teaches impulse control
* Motivation is fostered
* Dogs learn how to minimise stress
* Promotes wellbeing
* Strengthens health and prevents illness
* Anxiety is reduced (particularly in cases where there is fear of physical contact)

And we're off!
(practical exercises)

Where do I stand?

Dog Relax training will enable you to learn to become more in touch with yourself and to relax, allowing you to be much calmer when dealing with everyday life.

Practicing relaxation, and perhaps a few simple breathing or stretching exercises, stimulates the mind and body, promotes self-awareness, and reduces stress hormone levels. A natural flow is restored and a sense of wellbeing promoted, enabling you to behave in a more relaxed manner and think more clearly when making decisions. This is not just of benefit to you, of course, but also your dog.

As previously mentioned, every type of stress and tension you experience is picked up by your dog. Dogs are incredibly perceptive, and simply sense everything. When your behaviour is unambiguous, and you are expressing yourself more clearly and confidently, your dog will react to you as pack leader in an entirely different way, taking you seriously and accepting you completely.

Your new-found awareness and more sensitive body language will inevitably lead to an improvement in your posture, and you will feel as though you are standing straighter. The physical exercises within this book are particularly helpful for this, as they both relax and develop the back muscles.

The following sections provide you with instructions for standing steadfast and relaxed in everyday life; some physical exercises in order to prevent tension; details of a breathing technique, and a centring exercise using your hands. You will also find tips in the instructions for exercises for your dog.

Nothing can upset me – I'm as strong as an oak tree

Relaxation and breathing exercises help us to concentrate our energy and centre ourselves. A relaxed person will transmit a great deal of positive energy to his dog, and will simply find everything much easier.

I would now like to invite you to learn to relax. Let's begin with the 'tree relaxation.' (You will also find instructions for a breathing exercise, individual exercises for physical relaxation, and hints on reducing stress in your everyday life.)

Tree relaxation

The tree has become a very important element of my relaxation work. Humans feel drawn to trees; even primitive peoples held them in special regard.

The tree as symbol

A tree has roots that often reach deep into the earth, providing not only lifeblood, but also stability and security.

The trunk supports the tree and gives its visual character, allowing branches to grow that can tower into the sky.

So, make yourself comfortable and ensure that you won't be disturbed for a couple of minutes: no phone calls, no callers, etc.

Read through the following instructions a couple of times before beginning. When you have done the exercise once or twice, you will have memorised the sequence.

Take off your shoes and wear socks for this exercise. Stand with your feet about hip-width apart on a warm blanket. Wriggle your toes and then rotate your feet for a minute or two, then stop and stand still. Notice and be aware of your feet in contact with the floor.

Now imagine long roots growing out of your feet, which will provide you with security and stability, linking you to Mother Earth, who supports you throughout your life. Stay with this image for a moment, and enjoy the feeling of being supported by Mother Earth and infused with new vitality, which fills your whole body.

Focus on your legs and torso, and picture this as the solid trunk that supports you and holds you upright.

Imagine what your tree trunk looks like; its colour, bark structure, and size.

Stretch your arms to the sky whilst picturing the top of your tree reaching into the heavens. Feel the connection to the heavens, and to eternity. Notice how light you are feeling; very light and free.

Now focus on the strong connection of your roots downward to Mother Earth and the connection upward to the heavens and infinity.

Spend a moment enjoying the feeling that this picture gives you; the strength and solidity of Mother Earth and the effortless simplicity of the heavens.

You are a beautiful tree, completely but lightly connected to both heaven and earth, with a huge amount of strength flowing through your body; feel that energy.

You will take this feeling of stability and security with you into your everyday life, allowing your mind to be open and receptive to everything.

To finish, slowly lower your arms and let them hang loosely by your sides. Rotate your shoulders and move your legs, gradually becoming aware of the present moment.

Whenever you have a few spare moments, take the opportunity to assume your tree position: feel your connection to the Earth through your feet, and your connection to infinity through your arms.

This exercise is designed to ground you, promoting security and stability in your life; the intellectual connection to the heavens will give you increased mental clarity and creativity. (Simply looking up at the sky and letting your thoughts wander can be very relaxing ...)

The tree is a very powerful symbol; use its strength in your everyday life.

Fit and relaxed
Alternate nostril breathing to relieve stress and strain
The importance of breathing slowly and deeply has already been touched on in the previous section. In addition to concentrating on relaxed, free-flowing breathing, you can further support yourself by using the following special technique.

Sit in a comfortable position with your back straight
- Use your right thumb to press your right nostril closed. Your fingers will point upward to the ceiling. Breathe in and out through the left nostril (moon side)

After about two minutes, change nostrils and thumbs
- Now breathe in and out through the right nostril (sun side)

You will notice that one nostril will feel a bit blocked, as if you have a cold. This is the nostril on the side that is currently not very active and is having a bit of a 'break.'

Alternate nostril breathing for general relaxation (this is where it gets a bit more difficult)
- Breathe in through the left nostril – keep the right one closed
- Breathe out through the right nostril – keep the left one closed

This breathing exercise balances and relaxes the body.

The effect
Both nostrils are used to breathe in oxygen which is needed to live. However, the same amount is not breathed in and out at the same time through both nostrils, as one nostril always takes the greatest proportion of breath. This breathing dominance alternates between nostrils every 2-2.5 hours, ensuring that a balance of alertness and relaxation is maintained in the body.

Assistance from the sun and the moon
Deliberate left nostril breathing (moon side) induces relaxation and has a calming effect, which helps with restlessness and anxiety and, as Satya Singh writes in his book *Kundaliniyoga*, lowers blood pressure.

Right nostril breathing (sun side) has an energising effect which helps with tiredness and problems with concentration, and raises blood pressure (Satya Singh).

Alternative nostril breathing

Left nostril   Right nostril

Moon side: the moon represents the evening = peace and relaxation

Sun side: the sun represents daytime and warmth = strength, activity and alertness

Dog Relax

Body fit

The following physical exercises will liven you up, refresh your thoughts, relax your muscles, and have a 'de-stressing' effect.

Familiarise yourself with the exercises first, find out what suits you and which exercises link well with each other.

Bird flight

- Stand up straight but relaxed.
- Stretch out your arms in front of you and turn them so that the palms of your hands are facing each other
- Swing your arms behind you so that your hands touch. (To begin with the hands may not quite touch each other)
- Use the movement's natural impetus to swing your arms backwards and forwards, smoothly and not too fast

The effect

This is a good warm-up exercise, which also refreshes.

The chest is stretched and opened as the arms swing backward, creating a feeling of breadth and lightness. Breathing becomes deeper and tension between the shoulder blades loosens. The exercise has a refreshing effect and is beneficial after you have been sitting for a long time – say, in front of a computer – as it straightens the spine.

Exercises for the neck and shoulder area

The shoulder and neck area is very sensitive, and tends to tense up as a protective reflex when under stress.

Shoulder rolls

- Sit or stand with your back straight and slowly lift your shoulders towards your ears
- Holding this position, pull back your arms and shoulder blades, and then drop your shoulders in a circling movement

The effect

The entire pectoral girdle and chest area should be opened and loosened by the gentle circling movement, dissolving tension and correcting posture in the process. Another useful exercise after long periods spent sitting down.

Shoulder shrug

Sit or stand with your back straight and, in a decisive movement, lift your shoulders towards your ears and then immediately lower. Repeat briskly – up/down, up/down – twenty times.

The effect

Dissolves tension in the shoulder and neck area.
A dynamic exercise which opens up the bridge between the head and body.

Bird flight.

DOG RELAX

The owl – head movements

- Facing forward, turn your head very slowly to the left and look over your shoulder
- Then turn the head very slowly to the right, and look over the other shoulder
- Repeat this movement very slowly a couple of times
- Turn your head to face forward once more. Lift your head slowly and look at the ceiling (if you can)
- Finally, bend your head forward, bringing your chin down toward your chest
- Repeat this exercise very slowly a couple of times

The effect

If you spend a lot of time sitting down and have poor posture, the cervical spine and associated muscles very quickly become tense, causing pain. Stretching (dropping your chin down toward your chest) extends the neck muscles, which enables them to relax, allowing energy to flow again.

Please remember to do this exercise slowly, and only as many times as feels comfortable!

Owl' exercise.

Mudra practise: see page 54.

Fingertips
Finger relaxation (or mudra meditation)

Many magazines have articles on 'finger yoga:' pop stars, TV presenters and politicians do finger yoga. Whether it is practised consciously or unconsciously, the beneficial effect is evident.

The Sanskrit expression 'mudra' – a gesture, a particular position of the fingers – best describes finger yoga. Buddhas and other divine beings are generally depicted with various finger gestures or poses, each of which has a specific meaning. As well as Asia, mudras are used all over the world: giving someone the thumbs-up or joining your hands in prayer are examples of mudras from the western world. According to Chinese medicine, mudras work through the system of meridians; energy paths which run through the whole body, including the hands and fingers. In this respect, hands can be considered mirrors of our bodies in a similar way to foot reflexology. There are 4000 nerve fibres in the fingertips, which is what makes the mudras so effective. These nerve endings are in contact with our internal organs, and can settle and rebalance them via the brain.

Finger exercises can be carried out anywhere. Simply massaging your own hands and fingers is very beneficial, as it refreshes and relaxes your body and your mind, and stimulates the major organs via the hand reflex points.

Mudra practise
- Spread your fingers and place the fingertips of both hands together
- Hold your hands at chest height
- Hold this position for a short while

The effect

This mudra has long been practised to promote concentration; it is centring and has a relaxing effect.

This hand position is taught in management training; it's also common to see it used by TV presenters and politicians.

ACTIVE WELLBEING FOR YOUR DOG
Introduction

Now that we have looked at some relaxation exercises for you, here are some beneficial exercises for your dog.

I would once again like to draw attention to the need for patience and consideration when dealing with your dog. Practise only when you really want to and not just because you have scheduled it in your diary. Try to detect whether your dog is also in the right mood for the exercises; if he would rather snooze or sleep, it's better to leave him in peace.

If you want to make a start with the actual training, it's best if your dog is familiar with basic commands such as 'sit,' 'stand,' and 'down, stay;' and also with both visual and audible cues. If you are still at the level of practicing basic commands, you will need to be very patient. If you ask your dog for too much, too quickly, it may be that he will feel overwhelmed and lose interest. It is also important to bear in mind that not every day is the same. Something that might have worked yesterday can seem completely different today. *You* are also not in the same mood every day.

If your dog annoyed you yesterday, he has already forgotten all about it today, because dogs live in the here and now – in the present. They are highly developed social creatures, but do not live

Immie demonstrates the points of a dog.

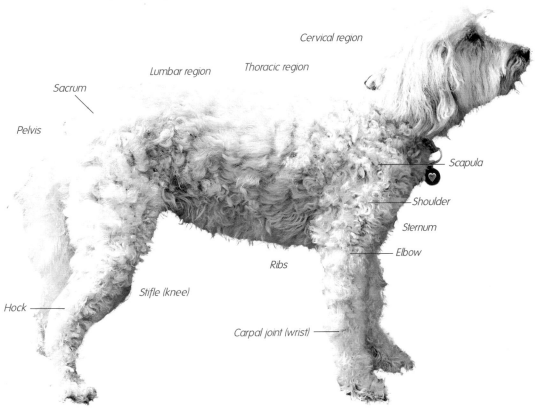

Cervical region

Lumbar region

Thoracic region

Sacrum

Pelvis

Scapula

Shoulder

Sternum

Elbow

Ribs

Stifle (knee)

Hock

Carpal joint (wrist)

or behave according to human morals or values. If your dog was angry yesterday (dogs also have emotions such as anger and rage), it's already history for him today. Revenge is alien to him and neither does he bear resentment. On the other hand, dogs behave very logically: in this respect, we humans can certainly learn something from our dogs!

Please train using positive reinforcement. Reward your dog after every success with praise and a treat. In some exercises, such as, for example, 'leg slalom,' the dog is enticed with a treat so that he can understand and link the direction of the movement. In other cases, give the reward only after a success, otherwise eventually your dog won't do anything without a treat! The point of the treats is to increase motivation; once the exercise has been mastered perfectly, you can minimise the number of treats you give.

Dog Relax active
- Remember that dogs are not machines, and experience different moods, just as we do
- Each time you train, make a note of your dog's mood and attitude
- Give him your full attention

Clicker training

It can be helpful to use a clicker when teaching certain exercises, as your dog can very quickly connect what he has done correctly with the click. More information on this method can be found in the many publications that cover this type of training.

- Progress step-by-step
- Mistakes and failures are allowed. Don't pressurise him to perform because this will generate stress

The following exercises are all designed to relax your dog's muscles and naturally prevent tension. The movements of each exercise are planned so that, in addition to stimulating the circulation and lymphatic system, they will also clear the meridians (see also the next chapter). The stretching and extension movements, and the relaxed body posture ensure that the muscles are stretched and the meridians activated.

Your dog should be warmed up before every stretching exercise. Play with him for a short time first, and massage his neck and back or groom him (you will find the instructions for a grooming massage in the section on massage), so that he doesn't strain or tear a muscle. This is particularly important for the 'dog yoga' and 'loose neck' exercises.

Please ensure that at the start you tackle each exercise individually. Combining two physical relaxation exercises should only be undertaken once you and your dog have completely mastered the exercises. After the exercises, you should massage your dog.

Be careful not to overtax your dog in any training session. A child of 5-7 years can concentrate for only 15 minutes at a time on average, so be just as considerate of your dog in this respect by practicing in very short bursts, followed by a play session.

Puppies and young dogs need to find out about the world through play first, in order to amass experiences for their future lives. For this reason, it's best not to worry too much about how perfectly your dog accomplishes the exercises; in, for example, 'As flexible as a snake,' too much intensive stretching should be avoided. With puppies, you should always focus instead on the wellbeing aspect.

Position

In the following exercise and massage instructions, you will be instructed to "assume a suitable position." This means that you should decide whether you want to stand, sit, kneel or squat on the floor, or stand by a table; if any other position is required, an explicit instruction will be given.

Another tip
Before you begin, read through the respective exercise – preferably a couple of times – and study the photos. Don't begin to practise with your dog until you have grasped the exercise sequence.

If you have back problems, it may be helpful to have your dog on a table (though ensure that he can't fall off). If you would prefer to work on the floor, sit, kneel or squat. Find whatever position is most comfortable for you.

It is very important not to scold your dog if the exercise sometimes doesn't go according to plan.

A relaxed neck
Exercise: head stretch left and right
- Stand at the side of your dog
- The dog is looking straight ahead
- Use a treat (from underneath the dog – see photo on page 60 – to get your dog to slowly turn her head back along the right side of her body, as if she wants to look toward her shoulder (head on one side, neck stretching close to the body)
- Return her head to the starting position
- Next, slowly guide her head to the left side, as previously described
- Slowly repeat this exercise: straight ahead – look to the right – straight ahead – look to the left – straight ahead – pause

Alternative version
This exercise can also be done with your dog in a sitting or lying position. If your dog is lying down, you must ensure that the pelvis stays straight and is not turned to one side as it is when she is lying in a relaxed position.

Important: Please ensure that your dog moves and stretches only her neck, with the back remaining as straight as possible. The exercise must always be done on both sides, very slowly and carefully.

The effect
This exercise increases mobility of the neck and the upper spine, loosens the dog's shoulder and neck muscles, and relaxes the shoulder blades.

This is an important stretching and relaxation exercise for dogs that pull on the lead, and therefore experience constant pressure in the throat and neck areas. Some dogs are so tense and

Head stretch.

toughened in the throat and neck areas from straining against the collar and lead that they have apparently become completely insensible to pressure, which results in more and more problems here. Recent research into the possible negative effects of too much pulling on a dog's neck and throat has shown that intra-ocular pressure can increase massively in the short-term.[1]

Having a relaxed throat and neck area is important because, in terms of energy, this region is a bridge between brain and body, with many peripheral nerves, energy channels, blood and lymph vessels running through it. Relaxed muscles here are of particular importance to enable everything to flow freely.

Tip
When it's necessary to have your dog on a lead, a chest harness, with a shock absorber, if required, is much kinder than attaching the lead to your dog's collar.

Once your dog is familiar with this exercise, you can progress to doing the 'cat and cow' exercise immediately afterward, which will mean that you have stretched the throat and neck in all four directions. The 'relaxed neck'

[1] Amy M Pauli, Ellison Bentley, Kathryn A Diehl, Paul E Miller (2006): Effects of the Application of Neck Pressure by a Collar or Harness on Intraocular Pressure in Dogs. (*Journal of the American Animal Hospital Association* 42:207-211 (2006).

Dog yoga: cow position.' Dogs with long necks find stretching easier.

massage is recommended for wellbeing in this area.

Dog yoga
Exercise: cat and cow for dogs

For the first part of the exercise ('cow' position):

- Begin with your dog standing quietly on the mat (it will obviously be beneficial in this instance if she is familiar with the 'stand' command)
- Stand next to her and place your hand under the back part of the abdomen so that she remains still
- Using a treat, entice her to gently stretch her neck and lift her head (see photo)
- Your dog's head and neck are now gently bent and pointing upward in the 'cow' position. Ensure that the stretching and movement happen slowly, and in a controlled manner, and never force the head backward in any way
- Keep your dog in this position for a couple of seconds, then allow her to lower her head and reward her with praise and a treat. Dogs with long necks find this stretch easier
- Change the position of your hands for part two of the exercise ('cat' position (see photo on page 64)
- Still with your dog standing, in order to keep the back as straight as

Dog yoga: cat position.'

> possible, place your arm directly behind her front legs as support for the rib cage
> * Again, using a treat, entice your dog to slowly lower her head between her front legs
> * By holding the treat in front of her nose, encourage your dog to gently and slowly stretch her neck in the opposite direction to the 'cow' position
> * Keep her in the 'cat position" for a couple of seconds and then reward as before

Once your dog is familiar with the cat position (head down), you can slowly and carefully increase the amount of neck stretch by holding the treat closer to the rib cage, thereby drawing her head further through her legs.

Tip

Make sure that you are very calm and quiet during the exercise, as it must be done very slowly to avoid any strain or alarm. In this respect, it is important that she does not make any sharp, sudden movements.

Once your dog has learnt each element of the exercise by practising them separately many times, you can combine the 'cow' and 'cat' movements to form one exercise, but be careful to change between the supporting hand and the rewarding hand for each.

Repeat the cat and cow position twice. When your dog has had some practise and is enjoying it, you can do it up to four or five times in a session. Always keep your four-legged friend in each position for a moment so that her muscles have a chance to extend and stretch.

If you and your dog like and are familiar with clicker training, you can use the clicker to train her into the positions, and then you won't need treats as enticements. However, this entails a more intensive practise schedule, and is only really suited to experienced trick trainers who have a lot of time and enthusiasm.

The effect

If the dog moves her head upward, the muscles under the chin are stretched and the neck muscles expanded. Getting up from her bed in the morning will make your dog stretch in this way (they know what is good for them ...).

Bending her head forward and through the front legs causes the neck muscles to stretch, which has a relaxing effect on the muscles at the front of her neck, an area that is often overstressed and tense from pulling on the lead. When a dog assumes the cat position, the muscles at the top of the back and the back extensor (a muscle that extends or straightens a limb or joint) are expanded. This is a very good relaxation exercise for all of your dog's neck, shoulder and back muscles. (Try it yourself and you will understand exactly how beneficial it is.)

Tip for humans

This is a traditional yoga exercise with a quick and positive effect. It relaxes all of the back muscles, increases spinal mobility, and stimulates lymphatic drainage, as a result of which, energy will flow more freely and vitality levels will rise. In turn, this will generate a feeling of wellbeing as the bladder meridian – the only meridian that is connected to all internal organs – is stimulated. Relaxed muscles are also much better for the nerve tracts that run along the spine.

Exercise: cat and cow for humans
- Get down on your hands and knees
- Cow position: lift your head slowly, and gently lower your lumbar area toward the floor
- Cat position: bend your head down between your arms and arch your back like a cat

Alternate these movements smoothly and gently. Keep your arms straight, and take care not to cross your feet.

The effect
This exercise will quickly relax your back muscles if you have been sitting for too long.

Bend and stretch yourself fit
Exercise: play bow
- With your dog standing, stand next to him
- Place one hand under the rear part of his abdomen to ensure that his rear end remains upright (this also ensures that he can't move forward)
- Move a treat to just in front of his forefeet so that he has to stretch his head down and forward, thus bending his front legs and placing the forearms on the ground/table in a play bow position. When your dog is in the correct position, reward him immediately with praise and a treat

This exercise can also be done very easily using a clicker. Each time your dog does as you ask, click and treat. In time, he will associate the click with the 'bow' command.

The effect
All animals have an innate love of stretching, and all dogs enjoy a good stretch in the morning or after a nap. A stretch extends through the whole body, including the throat and neck muscles, keeping ligaments and tendons mobile and flexible, and giving a feeling of wellbeing. In behavioural biology, luxuriating in a good stretch is interpreted as an expression of wellbeing, and associated with autogrooming behaviour.

Tips for advanced trainers
A perfect example of this exercise is when you simply assume the appropriate posture, make the relevant gesture, give the 'bow' command, and your dog bows in front of you. It can be helpful if you bow slightly at the same time, as then your dog will associate your movement with the exercise. Be patient and take whatever time is needed to ensure your dog has learnt the exercise properly. Your patience will pay dividends in the end, as your dog's perfect execution of the bow exercise will not only look impressive, but will also be good for him!

Practising the play bow.

DOG RELAX

Play bow: Benji immediately reacts to my hand gesture and posture.

Whilst I practise the play bow exercise with Benji, Amigo wakes up from his nap and enjoys a good stretch.

Santino enjoys a stretch of his own accord.

As flexible as a snake

Exercise: the slalom

Some dog owners will know this exercise from dog agility, where the dog slaloms through the weave poles, or from trick training, where the dog slaloms between her owner's legs. Few owners know that when done slowly or at medium speed, this is a beneficial and health-giving exercise for their dog.

　　Please note that this exercise is only suitable for healthy dogs. If your dog has any physical problems, please consult your vet before proceeding.

Version 1: slalom weave poles with or without a lead

- On a lead, guide your dog through a weave pole course. (The distance between the poles should be based on the size of your dog)
- Your dog should be nearest the poles, and should stay close to them so that she has to bend and stretch as much as possible to go round them (see photo below)

As I walk forward slowly, Benji snakes in and out of my legs.

Tip

Not every dog owner has weave poles, of course, but slalom cones (sold in toyshops) can be taken anywhere, and can be used to set up a slalom course.

Version 1 is of particular benefit to very small or very large dogs.

Version 2: between the legs slalom (see photo page 71)

You can practise this exercise with or without a clicker.

- Have your dog on your left-hand side, preferably sitting (because this encourages focus and calm)
- Step forward with your right leg, adjusting the size of your step to the size of your dog (small dog = small steps)
- Hold a treat in your right hand to entice your dog through your legs from the left; bring your right hand across the front of your legs and draw the dog from the left to the right side
- If your dog goes through your legs, reward her with praise and a treat, then ask her to sit and stay
- Step forward with your left leg and entice her through your legs with your left hand. Reward again with praise and a treat (and 'stop'). Your dog must sit and stay again to ensure that the exercise remains calm and controlled

Repeat these exercise sequences until your dog has understood that she has to thread herself in-between your legs.

Initially, practise left to right and stop, and then right to left and stop. Take a break.

Take your time very carefully and precisely practicing this short sequence. Once your dog has mastered this sequence, you can ask her to thread through your legs several times in a row until you have a flowing, slalom movement. When her movements have begun to flow, you can label the action with a vocal 'through' command, then you need only use this command and perhaps a visual cue to get your dog snaking around your legs. Go slowly wth this exercise: wth a little practise you can achieve a harmoniously flowing movement for human and dog, and need only reward with a treat after every second or third 'through.'

This second version can be rather hard on a person's back in the case of very small dogs, and some larger dogs find it difficult to walk comfortably between their owner's legs.

The effect

This slow-paced and relaxed slalom between the legs (which is different from the move used in dog agility) stretches the dog's entire body along both sides, as she has to bend to get around the poles or the legs. When she bends, the muscles along the outer side (away from the poles/legs) are stretched, as if the dog is making herself longer. The area between the shoulder and the pelvis is lengthened by the snaking movement, whilst the other side of the dog's body has to contract, which has a strengthening effect. The 'through the legs slalom' entails very tight bends, so the stretching is even more intense.

When done slowly, this is a very good exercise, which will stretch and strengthen the back and side muscles of the torso, and also the throat muscles. In addition, the back leg muscles are also strengthened, as the movement entails constant shifting of the dog's centre of gravity. The continually

Following my hand signals (right bend = right hand, left bend = left hand), Benji walks a figure of eight around and through my legs.

alternating left/right movement prompts the dog's brain to improve stimulus processing between its two halves, thereby teaching the sequence of movements through increased physical awareness. It also teaches physical coordination.

A figure of eight for your dog

Exercise: the figure of eight (see photo page 73)

If your dog has already learnt the 'as flexible as a snake' exercise, this next one should be very simple for him to learn.

Instead of doing a 'slalom,' your dog is asked to walk horseshoe bends, or a 'figure of eight' around your legs. This is similar to the 'as flexible as a snake' exercise, in that your dog will be going around your legs. This exercise is not very suitable for a very large dog, and may cause the owner back problems in the case of a very small dog.

- Stand in a straddle position and have your dog sitting on your righthand side
- With a treat in your right hand, lead your dog around the front of your right leg
- Take the treat in your left hand and encourage your dog to go between your legs
- Bring the hand with the treat around the back of your left leg and toward the front
- Your dog should follow the hand behind your left leg and to the front
- Switch hands again and lead your dog between your legs from the front and behind the right leg
- Once your dog has returned to the start position, ask her to sit and reward with praise and a treat

Tip

Your dog must keep very close to your legs when doing the figure of eight. Only reward when the complete figure of eight is achieved.

The aim should be that, after a period of intensive and patient training, your dog will be able to do a figure of eight around your legs by simply following your hand movements.

The effect

The effect is similar to that of the 'as flexible as a snake' exercise, although the bending and stretching is even more intense.

Alternative version

A variation on this theme would be for your dog to walk a figure of eight around two slalom cones, or other obstacles.

Sometimes it's good to go backward

Exercise: walking backward

- Stand directly in front of your dog, who should be standing
- Walk toward your dog so that he takes a step backward; if he doesn't quite understand what you want from him, use a treat to encourage him to go backward
- If your dog doesn't want to go backward by himself, simply press lightly with your fingers on his chest and gently push him back one step. Then reward him immediately with praise

and a treat. (Even if your dog is not inclined to go backward, the treat will motivate him to do so)

- Ask your dog to take another couple of steps backward, and then forward, ensuring that he doesn't walk in an arc. If you need to use a treat, hold it low so that he does not pull his neck up

    Please practise this with sensitivity – your dog must not feel threatened (this is very important in the case of insecure dogs).

Even the traumatised Greyhound lost his uncertainty about this obstacle,' and quickly understood the backward and forward movement.

Tip
In order to prevent your dog moving sideways to avoid doing the exercise, you can construct a barrier with two chairs (or with two large cardboard boxes). Let your dog have a look at your 'exercise equipment' first, so that he can get used to it before you attempt to use it with him.

Benji is following a treat backward here (he will also do this without the treat).

Practise so that your dog learns to go back a couple of steps when you use your chosen command (perhaps 'back'). Repeat the backward and forward exercise a couple of times, ensuring that he goes backward in as straight a line as possible

The effect
This exercise develops the dog's body consciousness and co-ordination, as by nature dogs generally would not choose to walk backward. The change in the centre of gravity that this exercise necessitates strengthens the muscles of the dog's rear end.

Alternative version

Your dog can also walk backward through your legs, as long as he is not threatened by you standing over him.

- Straddle your dog and gently entice him backward using a treat
- Ensure that you practise this with plenty of positive reinforcement

Look how tall I am!

Exercise: balance (see photo page 78)

Some dog training schools use balance wobble boards in their puppy play groups. Not every dog owner has access to these, and it's also important to do balance training with adult dogs (though less so with old dogs).

Give your dog's vestibular system (sense of balance and spatial awareness) some training. It is very important that you do this exercise on a non-slip surface.

- Depending on the size of your dog, either stand or kneel for this exercise
- Position yourself at the side of your dog. Bending from the knees, run your hands down her sides and inside the front legs
- With your forearms supporting her rib cage, carefully lift her. You can offer her a forearm to lean on (see photo on page 78)
- Your dog is now standing on her hind legs with her back as straight as possible
- If your dog is quite stable standing on two legs, you could also teach her to rear up on command and place her paws on your outstretched arm

Never pull your dog up by the paws. Dogs with back problems should not do this exercise. Small dogs often find the exercise very easy; larger dogs sometimes find it difficult. Please lift your dog very slowly and gently, and check that she is okay with it. You undoubtedly know your dog best: if she seems unsure or nervous, practise lifting her very gradually and in small increments, or postpone teaching this exercise until she has become used to the other exercises and massage, and gained confidence.

The effect

This exercise benefits the dog's vestibular system.

"If the vestibular system is not functioning steadily and correctly, the processing of other sensations becomes irregular and ambiguous, and the nervous system has difficulty really functioning smoothly."
– Jean A Ayres, psychologist and OT, 1998

Tip

When out on walks, let your dog walk along a fallen tree, balance on small walls, and walk on a variety of different surfaces, because every sensorimotor and motor stimulation is linked to the brain. These stimulating experiences will assist in the further development of the dog's nervous system. Balancing strengthens the back muscles, which are key to the body's stability.

This exercises and trains and stretches the dog's vestibular system.

Alternative version
If you have a small trampoline at home, this is also ideal for your dog to use, if she will. Simply standing on it will work those muscles involved in balancing.

It doesn't need to be a big trampoline; Teddy is having a lot of fun on this small one.

Wellness massage for your dog

WHAT MASSAGE DOES

Massage can be found in all cultures, and is a very old method of using touch to return harmony to troubled physiological functions, increase wellbeing, and support the healing process. Sometimes, massage is linked with certain techniques, or may be a case of simply 'laying on of healing hands.'

All massage has one thing in common: a positive effect at both physical and emotional levels. The simple act of laying hands on a patient ensures that he or she is more aware of this area. This method of learning to be more aware of oneself through others' hands is something that can be applied to both humans and animals. Touch enables relaxation and creates trust and closeness; very important benefits, particularly for anxious and nervous dogs, and those with behavioural problems. Research has proven that the brain of a creature which has experienced very little play and little contact is significantly underdeveloped.

Gentle massage has a very relaxing and refreshing effect. The Karolinska Institute in Stockholm has studied the use of touch and massage on animals, and has found that even a gentle wellbeing massage with only the fingers quickly promotes relaxation.

"The massage calmed the animals so much, it was as if they had received medication,"
– Kerstin Uvnäs-Moberg, physiologist from Stockholm. (Quelle Vital 11/2008)

The many millions of sensory cells in our skin register every touch and contact, regardless of how light it may be, and communicates it to the brain.

Neurophysiologist Håkan Olausson and a Swedish research team discovered that there are special nerve tracts in the body that are responsible for sending a message about touch and stroking to the brain. These signals go straight to the limbic system, the part of the brain that manages the emotions.

Affectionate touching aids intelligence and brings about a biochemical reaction in our body by causing the release of the hormone oxytocin. This hormone has demonstrable benefits: circulation is improved and blood pressure lowered, stress hormone levels are reduced, and the immune system is activated, all quickly resulting in a feeling of wellbeing.

"A dog's oxytocin levels rise when his owner pets him, and petting his dog raises the owner's oxytocin, too."
– Temple Grandin, author, 2007

The beneficial effect on the dog owner is described in detail by Dr Carola Otterstedt in *Menschen brauchen Tiere (Humans need animals)*.

In his research, Dr Seymour Levine observed that rats which had been touched very little or not at all during their early development suffered severe consequences: the way that their nervous systems reacted to external stimuli was permanently altered. In contrast, those animals which had been cared for and touched showed far less anxiety and fear when under stress, and also demonstrated different behaviour as adults. Their hormonal stress system was checked, which protected the animals from an escalation of the chemical stress reaction.

Touch is therefore a very important factor in positive development. For this reason, tactile stimulation and social affection have a positive effect on stress reduction.

Oxytocin: the cuddle hormone

The release of the hormone oxytocin is important for wellbeing and harmony. Oxytocin plays an important role during childbirth and milk production, and also throughout life, as it is the 'cuddle hormone.' Stroking is calming, and this is as true for the animal kingdom as it is for humans.

During stroking, special pathways transmit stimuli to the brain and trigger a cascade of positive feelings. Blood circulation is stimulated, production of cortisol, the stress hormone, is reduced, and the emotional connection to the human doing the stroking is intensified.

Dr Ursula Zimmermann, veterinarian

The beneficial effects of massage
- Blood and lymph node circulation stimulated, producing a detoxifying effect
- Reflective effect on the flow of energy (meridians)
- Stress reduction: physical and mental relaxation
- Tactile stimulation and regulation of muscle tone
- Creation of inner equilibrium (particularly in nervous dogs)
- Tense muscles loosened

- Fosters feelings of security and trust
- Strengthens the bond between human and animal

An especially relaxing effect can be experienced by dogs which have assumed a posture that is physically unnatural and restrictive as a result of emotional injury or traumatic experience, as this poor posture can lead to very tense muscles. The same effect can be seen in stressed or anxious people who tend to tense their neck and shoulders. Body cells can store memories, which, if retained, result in muscle tension. For this reason, it is very important to stroke and massage areas of the body that are showing signs of muscle tension, so that these 'old memories' can be lovingly stroked away.

Not only are the muscles stimulated and strengthened during a massage; so, too, are the associated nerve cells, the spinal cord, and the brain.

Dog Relax wellness massages are designed to instil a feeling of wellbeing in your dog, but note that they are really only to be used at specific times. Please remember that neither human or dog wants to be constantly fondled and fussed over, and dogs do not appreciate being touched without warning.

Always touch your dog very gently, attentively and affectionately; some people have to learn this type of touching as it's not only children who like to grab! Ensure that you are particularly careful around the dog's head, and don't thoughtlessly stroke her over the eyes. Train your instinct and your intuition to determine where and how your dog likes to be touched.

The more often you deliberately stroke or touch your dog, the quicker you will get to know which muscles are tense. Those with no prior experience of dog massage should begin with the 'flowing hands' massage. When you are doing this, try to be very aware of how your dog's body feels under your hands. Virtually everyone has stroked a dog, but probably not consciously perceived it and sensed how the dog is really responding. Younger dogs sometimes seem almost addicted to touch, whilst older ones like to be left in peace more. Take care to observe what your dog's needs are at any one time before proceeding.

Dogs can react with tactile defence, ie: they may have a negative reaction to touch. The primate researcher Harry Harlow proved that monkeys which grew up with no physical contact became shy

or even aggressive. It can also be the case that dogs who were taken away from their mother very early, or which have had very few pleasant early tactile experiences may not have the necessary brain development to appreciate touch and contact. These animals may always have difficulty accepting tactile stimulation, whether in the form of grooming, massage, or simple stroking.

Insecure or nervous dogs find it more difficult to be receptive to this: in my work with rescued dogs, experience has shown me that it can sometimes take a year or even longer before the dog becomes completely receptive. Be particularly patient and forbearing, and the time will come when your dog happily offers you his tummy to stroke. If for some reason this doesn't happen, however, then you can use the 'magic points' or 'energy lines' for an alternative version, with your dog lying on his side. Please do not ever turn a dog onto his back against his will in order to get to his tummy.

Fluse and Celia touching muzzles and relaxing together.

Massage your dog only when he is feeling comfortable and is completely healthy. If he is unwell, simply resting your hand on him is enough, and he should happily accept this contact.

The significance of the meridians

The dog's circulatory system is constantly moving blood and lymph fluid around the body, together with another 'electrical energy.'

Over 5000 years ago the Chinese discovered that the body is traversed by pathways through which there is a constant flow of a small amount of electrical energy. These energy pathways are known as meridians. They are integrated with the organs and the body surface to form a single entity, and are the focus of traditional Chinese medicine (TCM), and other treatments originating in Asia, such as acupuncture and acupressure. The Chinese believe that the energy pathways convey the 'Qi' through the body, thereby supplying vital energy to every area. The Indians call this energy 'Prana' and the founder of classical homeopathy, Samuel Hahnemann, created the term 'life energy.'

When the life energy can flow freely through the meridians, both human and animal feel healthy and happy. If, however, the flow of energy is interrupted, there can be physical and emotional trouble. The notion that emotions can be therapeutically influenced by stimulating the acupuncture points is as old as acupuncture itself; around 5000-6000 years. This (life) energy and energy stimulation has nothing to do with New Age thinking, as the Japanese scientist Dr Hiroshi Motojamas proved the physical existence of these acupuncture points back in the 1970s. In 1989, the University of Witten/Herdecke announced the following sensational news: Prof Dr Hartmut Heine had photographed the specific points under the microscope, which meant that the acupuncture points could therefore be categorised.

There are established acupuncture and acupressure points on the meridians which relate to certain internal organs and their function. In the 1920s, American doctor Frank Chapmann discovered the neurolymphatic reflex system with its massage points that activate the lymph system, thereby stimulating the entire body. We have the Californian chiropractor Terrence Bennet to thank for the discovery of the neurovascular reflex point (Bennet reflex points) on the head, which influence blood supply to individual organs. Chiropractor John Goodheart linked these reflexes with the muscular system. This work was refined by Dr George Goodheart, founder of applied kinesiology, and Dr John Diamond, originator of behavioural kinesiology. Some doctors and vets have integrated kinesiology into their area of work. Inner equilibrium can be restored very quickly with a few physical exercises, and by patting, rubbing or holding the acupressure points, or the neurolymphatic or neurovascular reflex points.

Some of these points – those that increase a feeling of wellbeing in a dog – are mentioned in the following text, but remember that the aim of this book is not to advise on curing illness by touching or stroking certain acupressure points – that must be done by an expert.

Dos and don't of massage

Never massage your dog when he is unwell, or has any inflammations, sores or injuries.

Pregnant bitches should only be touched very gently, and there should be no stimulation whatsoever of any reflex areas.

If your dog is unwell, has diarrhoea, or an infection, then please leave him in peace.

Ensure that your dog has somewhere quiet to rest after any operation, and simply lay your hands on him.

Older dogs can sometimes be very fussy about how they like to be touched.

PREPARATION
Touch
Deliberately touching a dog in order to do him some good doesn't cost anything: you need only time, motivation, and consideration. Young puppies already love relaxing, and enjoy stroking and massage, both of which reduce stress. In fact, puppies in the neonatal stage would have little chance of survival without the stimulation of being licked by their mother; loving care that is their earliest form of social contact.

For young dogs, touching is a kind of social interaction, although older dogs also demonstrate such behaviour with close contact, social grooming, and tender touches with their muzzles when they have an attachment to each other. When we stroke a dog, this emulates the social grooming behaviour of canines amongst their own kind.

DOG RELAX

Affectionate physical contact between human and dog is important, and has a big influence on the positive social behaviour of the animal (as well as the human!). The aim is that the dog should experience something positive as a result of being touched by the human. Most dogs enjoy this contact and offer their stomach for stroking.

Social body care in the form of tender touching.

"Offering the stomach and throat can even initiate grooming behaviour as carried out by canine parents on puppies, ie: stomach massage with the tongue and a stimulating massage of the excretory organs." – Eberhard Trumler, author, 2004

Social grooming doesn't just groom, it also reduces aggression, acts as reassurance, and maintains social relationships.

When you begin to work with a young dog, be very patient, and don't expect too much from him. Gently and affectionately acclimatise your dog to your stroking before you begin to massage. A young dog can very quickly learn that there is a place – the special mat – where he can relax. He can lie down and will then be gently stroked, which is the best of treatments for puppies. This contact also stimulates the puppy mentally.

This approach can also be used with dogs that have not been used to stroking, but remember that there will be times when a dog may not want to be touched.

"A large amount of trust is a prerequisite for touching the head in particular. Stroking the head and cheeks, touching the eyes and lips ... has multiple facets from consolation to tenderness, but they are all linked to a great degree of intimacy in the relationship." – Samy Molcho, body language expert 2006

It is precisely for this reason that we should also show our dogs the same respect that we show other people. A dog has the same right, but sometimes his reaction to those who fail to take this into account is usually misinterpreted. From today, ensure that you touch your dog carefully, attentively, and with respect.

Discover what kind of contact your dog prefers. Does he remain relaxed when you stretch his legs? Are there areas or certain types of contact that seem to confuse him, make him tense, or even panicked? When you notice that your dog is feeling uncomfortable, respect that: perhaps he is not yet ready for that particular sort of contact, or perhaps he simply doesn't like it.

What sort of massage you give will depend to a certain extent on the type of dog you have. A large, powerful animal, such as a St Bernard, will prefer more vigorous stroking than would a Chihuahua. A Sharpei, with his many folds of skin, will need a different approach than will a Greyhound, for example, and long- and short-haired dogs require different types of massage. Don't stroke long-haired breeds too firmly against the direction of hair growth, as some don't like this. It may help to brush a long-haired dog before beginning a massage, as then your fingers will glide more smoothly through the coat. In all physical contact with your dog, be informed by your feelings, your awareness, and your intuition. Although it may take a while to fine-tune, sense what your dog likes; how and where he would like to be touched, and match the strength, technique and firmness of your touch to his needs.

*Ghalah's grooming
session with her pups.*

*Zissy giving a stomach
massage; her puppy is
obviously enjoying it.*

DOG RELAX

In my Dog Relax training courses, all of the massages are tried out on humans first. In this way, dog owners get to experience for themselves what a massage feels like, and how quickly a feeling of wellbeing is generated. In addition, you also appreciate when a massage begins to feel unpleasant because of too much pressure, or movements that are too fast.

Massage relieves muscle tension, which can disrupt the delicate balance within the body. Simple movements, such as firm strokes, can minimise the tension and enable everything to 'flow' freely again.

A walk beforehand, or an extensive play session, should ensure that your dog has burned off any surplus energy and is relaxed.

Stroking
Place your hands gently on your dog and stroke up and down with them (as in the 'flowing hands' massage)

Canine signals

Look out for the subtle signals that your dog sends you during a massage. It may be a change in facial expression, luxurious stretching, a deep sigh, or wanting to withdraw.

There are many signals that he may give, so train yourself to watch for them.

Dogs do not like to have their heads touched roughly.

DOG RELAX

Drawing squiggles
Using your thumbs or fingertips, move slowly down the back, lightly 'drawing' circles on both sides of the spine

Circles
Lay your hands on flat and make gentle circular movements

Palpating and kneading
Palpate a specific area and knead lightly – this is the technique for paw massage, for example

Effleurage
This technique can be used in tail massage, moving from the back to the end of the tail with long, gentle strokes. The ears can also be smoothed with long strokes

Caterpillar walk
Make small twisting movements with the thumbs, like a caterpillar creeping along

Petrissage
Lightly knead the neck muscles

Finger pressure
Acupressure massage should be carried out with the thumb or the index finger. Take care to ensure that your fingertip is in a relaxed position and has a short fingernail. Apply gentle pressure with your fingertip

Stroking and massage are a wordless conversation. Feel your dog's emotions and enjoy this time in complete silence.

THE RELAXATION STATION
Choose a special blanket or yoga mat to use for Dog Relax relaxation training, and use it only for this, so that your dog comes to appreciate its significance.

My yoga mat is my dogs' favourite thing. When I spread it out to do yoga myself, the dogs get on it before I can! After I have done my exercises, I am happy to massage my dogs. They know exactly what is going on ... Whilst I do my exercises, one of them is usually lying close by and waiting to see whether relaxation is on his timetable that day.

So, firstly, get your dog used to the blanket: let her look it over and lie on it if she wants to. It can be helpful to do a couple of gentle, relaxing back exercises yourself before you begin, letting go of your everyday thoughts, and taking a few long, deep breaths. Savour the feeling of relaxation. Get into a comfortable position. Quietly call your dog to you and perhaps offer a treat.

It's important that your dog doesn't think she is about to play a game, so, whilst she eats the treat, stroke her and maybe get her to lie down on the blanket. After doing this a few times, your dog will quickly connect this relaxed mood with the blanket. Only practise when you really have time, otherwise any tension will be communicated to her. This massage time belongs to your dog, so create a calm atmosphere that won't be disturbed. During the massage, your dog should feel completely secure and safe, so be careful not to abuse this trust. Be very attentive to your dog's needs; never alarm her during the massage by doing something thoughtless.

Remain relaxed when performing the massage. Radiate calm and composure. When you spread the relaxation blanket with the right frame of mind, this will create a positive atmosphere that your dog will welcome.

Rub your hands together to warm them and get the energy flowing, then begin to touch your

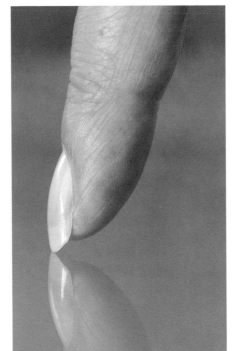

This fingernail is clearly too long.

Completely unposed: as soon as I unroll my relaxation blanket, my dogs arrive and take up their places!

dog by gently stroking her. Don't position her in any way which may cause tension. Ensure that she remains very relaxed; if she has an unsettled reaction or tries to draw away, find a position that she does feel comfortable in. If necessary, stop the acclimatisation phase for that day and carry on with the practise another time – this is particularly important for dogs who are very nervous or unsure, or who have had traumatic experiences. These cases require a great deal of patience and love. Some dogs have to acclimatise to being touched at all, initially, not because they are unsure and anxious, but because they have never had experience of being touched, and these may resist initially, or try to withdraw. Again, much patience on your part is required.

If your dog remains very relaxed, place your hand or hands on her; feel her heartbeat. This is where the health and relaxation experience begins.

More tips before you get started
When you massage your dog, she should quickly relax. It is important, however, that you also feel comfortable whilst carrying out the wellness massages so that you don't become tense. If health issues prevent you from sitting on the floor, you can certainly lay the relaxation blanket on a table and make this your 'relaxation station' for this special time.

Never suddenly or abruptly break off stroking or massage, as this always feels very unpleasant for the person (or animal) being touched. Always end a massage by letting your hands rest on the dog's body for a short while, before slowly withdrawing them. Afterward, give your hands a good shake to relax them.

Flowing hands
- Ask your dog to lie on her side on the relaxation blanket
- Sit in a position that you will be comfortable in for a while
- Your dog's back should be facing you (once she comes to know this massage she will remain in position)
- With your dog lying quietly, lightly lay your hands on her (ensure that you have warmed them first). Place your hands somewhere in the middle of her body
- Now feel the contact with your dog; be consciously aware of her
- Take long, deep breaths, quieten your thoughts and try to switch off
- Trust your hands' 'knowledge' and allow them to flow over the whole of your dog's side. You can make long stroking movements or gentle circles: be creative! Your hands can move synchronously or separately; keep moving and don't stay in one area
- Let your hands move over her legs, tail, ears and – very carefully – her head (but don't ever stroke over her eyes)
- Stay in physical contact with your dog and be receptive to her signals. Where does she particularly enjoy being touched? What does she seem to find less pleasant?
- Your dog will soon be feeling very relaxed
- After a few minutes, gently turn your dog onto her other side and repeat the procedure. As some dogs actually fall asleep during this massage, give her a brief signal before turning her over, to avoid alarming her
- To finish, let your hands rest on the dog and leave them there for a moment or two. Slowly lift them from her body
- Let your dog remain lying for a while, then gently stroke her from the middle of her head, along her spine to the end of the tail
- Allow your dog to slowly stand or remain lying down, as she wishes
- Guide her gently back into everyday life

The effect
'Healing hands' is a concept often mentioned in relation to massage, and, as is the case with massage, you will be in contact with your dog physically and in terms of energy. Stroking both

Flowing hands: human and dog become as one.

sides of your dog's body has a relaxing and warming effect, encourages circulation, and stimulates the muscles and underlying tissue. The strokes target the more sensitive nerves, lymph flow is stimulated, and muscular tension dispersed and dissolved.

Simultaneously, this massage promotes trust and deepens attachment, and your dog learns to accept stroking with complete confidence (which also makes grooming and processes such as checking for ticks much easier).

Tip for humans

It is hard to describe the deep, relaxing and luxurious effect of this massage. Try lying on your stomach and ask your partner or a friend to move their 'flowing hands' on your back: you will feel, experience and understand why your dog will enjoy this massage.

Relaxed neck

Remove your dog's collar: he can either sit or lie down, but it is best if you can reach his neck from behind him. (Attempting this massage from the side is not a very good idea.)

- Place your hands on the side of your dog's neck, and gently but firmly knead the large muscle groups from the upper neck down to the shoulder blades. Remember to keep movement direction downward, working from the top to the bottom (because of lymphatic flow)

- Massage the muscles at the side of the neck as well as the shoulder muscles, and those at the back/base of the neck (the trapezius, sternocephalic and brachiocephalic muscles)

- In the area of the dog's withers, use both thumbs to massage each side of the spine, centimetre by centimetre. (This is the location of the relaxation points of the bladder meridian)

    Don't massage the spine!

- Then place your thumbs directly on the

Kneading: gently kneading the neck provides an important feelgood massage for your dog.

base of the skull to the left and right of the spine and either press gently on or circle lightly around these neurolymphatic points for a moment – see photo below – but note that this is an extremely sensitive area

- From the base of the skull, move your thumbs in small gentle movements (as a caterpillar would walk) on the muscles next to the spine. Work your way down to the shoulders
- Finish with 2 or 3 long strokes from the base of the skull to the shoulder blades, as if you were drawing two lines next to the spine with your thumbs

Never massage the spine directly. Match the intensity of your massage to the type and size of dog (a St Bernard will definitely like a firmer massage than would, say, a Toy Poodle).

The effect
Many dogs have never been taught to walk properly on a lead, so they often actually 'hang' on it, and the resultant pull on the collar very often causes neck tension. The neck is an 'energy bridge' between head and body, and contains peripheral nerves, blood and lymph vessels, plus a main

meridian. If a large amount of tension builds up in this area, it can have unfortunate consequences for the dog's health (see also 'relaxed neck').

Important
If you notice something unusual in this area, or your dog reacts with extreme sensitivity, please consult a vet or a veterinary osteopath.

Crystal energy
Researchers have recently investigated the scientific evidence behind crystal healing therapy. According to Michael Gienger, founder of crystal healing therapy in Germany, gemstones have a positive effect on humans, and there's no reason why they shouldn't do the same for dogs!

As my test subjects (my dogs) show a very positive reaction to this therapy, I would like to recommend this type of massage.

You will need 'gentle' semi-precious stones. For example: white quartz and rose quartz are both said to emit sensitive vibrations. Rose quartz is reputed to open the heart and provide support in times of confusion and anxiety.

Rose quartz massage
Use an egg-shaped stone for this massage. It should be about 5-6cm (2in) long, and fit comfortably in your hand.
- With your dog lying relaxed on the mat/blanket, find a comfortable position next to her. Hold the rose quartz egg in your hand for a couple of minutes first to warm it, then gently place the long side of the egg on her body (see photo on page 100)
- Gently glide the stone up and down the side of your dog's body, or move it in circles. Imagine that you are painting your dog with the stone, and allow your imagination and your movements free rein, whilst using as your template the area in blue on the photo, page 101

Important: Never directly massage your dog's spine!

- Moving backward from the neck area, begin to make a 'rib pattern' with the tip of the egg, as if tracing your dog's ribs – see the red lines on the bottom photo, page 101. 'Draw' each line from the spine to the stomach
- Then turn your dog onto her other side and repeat the procedure
- Finish by drawing the tip of the egg 3 times down each side of the dog's spine from her neck to the base of her tail
- Lay the egg on its side and gently, without pressure, draw it directly up the spine from the base of the tail to the dog's head
- Slowly remove the stone
- Finish the session quietly, with your dog in the 'down' position, or remaining where she is for a time

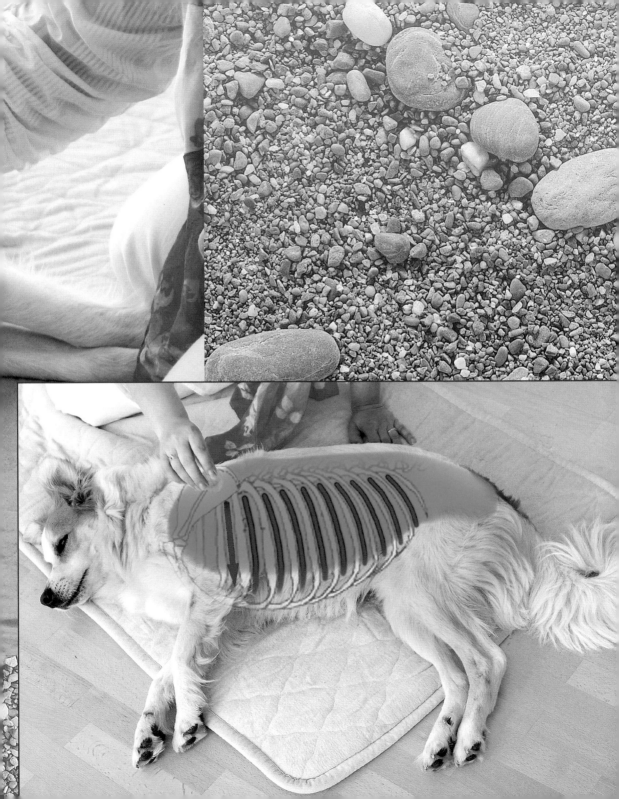

DOG RELAX

The effect

The rose quartz boosts the effect of the massage, which dissolves muscular and energy blockages, and induces a feeling of wellbeing. (Humans love this massage, too!)

White quartz massage

You can do this massage with either two round white quartz palmstones, or with milky quartz.

- Ask your dog to sit, and then find a comfortable position behind him
- Take a white quartz stone between each thumb and forefinger, and place these gently on their sides on the dog's body
- Now begin to stroke the crystals in a circular motion over the whole of the dog's back and neck area, but don't massage the spine. Some dogs also love this gentle massage behind their ears and on their heads, but be very careful when stroking this area
- Do a short massage at first, and, over time, increase the duration according to the needs of your dog. Start with the back area initially and include the head at a later stage

The effect

Similar to that of the rose quartz massage, with a high level of relaxation and feeling of wellbeing.

Tip for humans
The rose quartz massage is a treat for humans, and not just of benefit to the back. The white quartz massage is recommended for the head area in humans. Treat yourself to a gentle head massage with white quartz. Simply stroke the stones all over your head; you'll enjoy it!

Hedgehog balls
If you have a hedgehog ball in the house, you can make your dog feel 'hog happy'
- With your dog standing, sitting, or lying on her side (although it is, of course, more relaxing if she lies down), move the hedgehog ball gently over the side of her body, but not her head. If your dog likes it, you can also massage the legs, although it may be that this area is too sensitive

The effect
Hedgehog ball massage offers all of the benefits of a standard massage. In addition, tactile stimulation, lymphatic drainage, and the body's circulation are also boosted. The 'spines' on the hedgehog ball massage the muscles, and this quickly induces a feeling of wellbeing. The hedgehog ball is a tool for massage and for training in awareness, but not for grooming.
Adjust the amount of pressure you use to the breed/size of dog. There are several different sizes of hedgehog ball.

Grooming
In behavioural biology, all of an animal's activities directly related to body care are described as comfort behaviour or autogrooming:
- You can combine a pleasant grooming massage with a check for parasites
- Use whichever massage brush or curry comb is suitable for your dog/type of coat. In the case of small dogs, use smaller massage brushes, and touch your four-legged friend with appropriate care. Larger, stronger dogs often love coarser massage brushes with knobbles that can be stroked over the body. Obviously, which brushes and combs you choose to use for the grooming massage depend on the length and coarsness of your dog's coat
- If you're unsure which tool to use, get some advice from a specialist pet care shop. With massage brushes, please ensure that the ends of the pins have bubble tips to protect your dog's skin. (Grooming tools can often be bought cheaply in equestrian supplies stores)

The effect
(Mutual) grooming is social behaviour, and promotes social bonds. In China, tapotage (tapping) all over the body is very popular among humans, as it loosens the muscles and stimulates tactile perception, and also invigorates energy flow (the meridians). It is certainly possible to perform gentle tapotage with a cupped hand on a dog, though it's important to only do this if the dog allows and enjoys it. However, you can immediately begin combining grooming and the invigorating effect of tactile physical stimulation in a refreshing grooming massage.

Benji loves the hedgehog ball!

Tip
There are a few breeds of dog which it is not possible to groom using a brush. In these cases, simply use your fingertips to stimulate the dog's skin.

Relaxing strokes for your dog
In traditional Chinese medicine, various methods – such as acupuncture – are used to harmonise energy in the meridians and encourage it to flow freely. From this, applied kinesiology then developed another method of harmonising, stimulating or calming chi energy: gentle massage or tapotage is applied to specific reflex points or zones.

To achieve a reduction of emotional stress, some neurovascular reflex zones – most of which can be found on the head – are gently touched.

These reflex zones are also known as 'stress reduction points' or 'happiness points.' This exercise can be done anytime and anywhere.

A selection of massage brushes.

- Gently touch your dog's head
- Place your hand on his head and begin to gently press on the reflex zones with your thumb and forefinger (see photo on pages 106 & 109), or gently massage the reflex zones with small circular movements

Please note
The location of these areas will depend on the shape of your dog's head (a Greyhound's head is a different shape to that of a Chihuahua or a Papillon).

If your dog has a very sensitive head, be very gentle and perhaps limit yourself to lightly stroking his head at first, progressing to the reflex zones next time. Do not ever stroke too close to the eye sockets as dogs find this very unpleasant.

The effect
There are many nerve endings, acupuncture points, and reflex zones on the head. Applying emotional human stress reduction zones to dogs, the points where your.thumb and forefinger are

circling are the 'neurovascular reflex points,' the stimulation of which quickly produces a relaxing effect, and can minimise feelings of insecurity, stress-based excitement, and anxiety. This also relaxes dogs very quickly.

Opposite, top: An Irish Wolfhound enjoys being groomed, attentively watched by puppy Elsa.

"Improved circulation in the frontal lobes impedes the fight or flight mechanism, and enables new reactions to problematic situations." – from the script "A basic course in kinesiology" by Birgit Fuchs

Examples of when to use
- My Podenco used to become very over-excited when he met people and dogs. The 'relaxing strokes' enabled him to learn to stay quiet and relaxed in these situations. Initially, I had to touch the relaxation points frequently, but then less and less
- Using the 'relaxing strokes' very quickly helped an extremely traumatised and nervous Greyhound – who stared fixedly and seemed almost emotionally numb – to relax and enjoy a feeling of wellbeing. Right from the start, he was happy to submit to the 'relaxing strokes,' and sometimes it even seemed as it he was asking for them! The physical contact involved was very important for this dog, and helped reduce the extremely high level of tension, and incidence of the frozen stare.

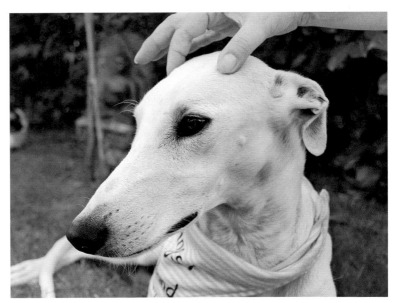

Tip for humans
You can stimulate these areas on yourself anytime (and anywhere) in order to relax quickly in stressful situations. This also helps with anxiety and restlessness, and problems with concentration.

In humans, the neurovascular points are found on the forehead, on the frontal eminence. You can find them by placing your thumb and forefinger on the mid-point of your eyebrows and then gently gliding your fingers up your forehead until you feel the 'mounds' or 'frontal eminences:' never in the hairline; that is too far up (see photo, opposite).

Magic points
'Magic points' are acupressure points that, when stimulated, can produce a positive feeling in the dog. The points should be pressed or touched very gently, or perhaps stimulated with a gentle circling motion in order to promote the body's natural powers of self-healing. Pressing on these points dissolves muscular tension, and quickly induces relaxation, and a feeling of wellbeing on an

Opposite, bottom: It's not possible to groom a Bergamasco Sheepdog like Chira with a brush.

A Greyhound's head is a different shape to that of a Chihuahua or a Papillon.

emotional level. Michael Gach has written about these 'healing points,' which, when pressure is applied, release endorphins (pain-relieving neurotransmitters). Pain is blocked and more blood and oxygen is transported to the affected area, which in turn ensures that the muscles relax.

Obviously, never press on fresh scars.

Kidney point NI 27

Location: the depression each side between the first rib and the lower edge of the clavicle (see photos, pages 110/111).

- Gently massage these two points, preferably with the thumb and forefinger of one hand, with the other hand on the dog's navel area

The effect

Kidney point NI 27 is a very important stress reduction point in humans, and I have also experienced very positive outcomes after holding or gently massaging this point in dogs. Stimulating these reflex points causes the underlying arteries to expand, thus supplying the brain with more oxygen and

blood sugar. There is also an increase in the release of neurotransmitters, and in the flow of electro-magnetic energy, which improves the performance of the brain and clears the head. (Source: *Basic course in kinesiology*, Birgit Fuchs, naturopath.)

These reflex zones in dogs are hardly mentioned by experts, but this is probably because, like auricular (ear) acupuncture, it is a relatively new area, but, again, there's no reason why we shouldn't use these neurolymphatic reflex zones on the dog.

Tip for humans
Massage both of your own NI 27 points using your thumb and index finger. You will find these points under your clavicle, near to the sternum. Rub your navel with your other hand.

Prof Dr Franz Decker states that massaging the acupuncture points on the kidney meridian has a very fast stress-reducing effect. The kidney meridian is associated with the fear emotion.

Stimulate these points for feelings of anxiety; helps with centring and boosts concentration.

Pelvis energy line KG 6
See the photo on page 122 for the location of KG 6 on the meridian. Massage this area with a gentle circling movement.

The effect
General reinvigorating effect for states of exhaustion.

Pelvis energy line KG 17
Location: the centre of the sternum, level with the first pair of nipples (see photo page 112). Massage with a gentle circling movement.

The effect
Helps reduce levels of fear or anxiety; also assists when emotional stability has been disrupted.
　　KG 17 is a central point where the heart, lung, spleen, liver, kidney and triple warmer meridians intersect. It is a point with a strong influence on the Qi (life energy).

Energy line of the brain
Leader energy line points LG 18 + 19
Location: See photo page 113 for the location of LG 18 + LG 19: massage lightly.

Dog Relax

The effect
LG 18: calms agitation.
LG 19: helps relieve neck tension.

Leader energy line point LG 20
Location: The highest point on the head (in some animals you can feel a slight bump in the bone

here, particularly in the case of Greyhounds). Touch or gently massage this point for a moment (see photo below).

The effect
LG 20 has a mildly sedative and calming effect, which will help with general restlessness and anxiety; it is also said to have a positive effect on the pituitary gland. This point can be used to quickly balance energies. Stimulation has a relaxing effect; this area is also known as the 'point of one hundred meetings.' In humans, depression is helped. Most dogs love being touched here.

If you have a Chihuahua, please note that, in some, the fontanelle never closes, a small hole remaining in the top of the skull that is covered by skin only. Ensure that you avoid these points if this is the case with your dog.

Leader energy point LG 24.5
Location: Between the eyes but a little higher: touch or gently massage this point. (see photo below).

Dog Relax

The effect

Relaxes the central nervous system. Use to calm nervousness and over-excitement, and provide support where there is anxiety.

Other energy points on the conception vessel (KG) and the governing vessel (LG) are described in the section on 'energy lines.'

Mood barometer

Exercise: Making a long tail

- The aim is to loosen and stretch the tail and associated muscles
- Your dog should be standing in a comfortable position. Start with the muscular area at the bottom of the back (gluteal muscles) and massage – perhaps lightly knead – around the base of the tail with your thumb and fingertips. Do not, however, massage on the spine.

Depending on the breed of dog, you can also use your whole hand to gently massage with circular movements on larger and more muscular dogs.

- Both marked areas (2 and 3, shown as blue spots in the photo opposite) can be massaged with gentle circular movements. Tension often builds up in the muscles in these areas
- Carefully stroke both thumbs next to the spine from the mid-back to the base of the tail. If your dog enjoys this, repeat a couple of times
- Then take the tail in your hand (or hands, if it is a large dog), and very gently 'roll' it 2-3 times in each direction
- Next, let your hand lightly glide a couple of times from the base of the tail to its tip. Pull very gently whilst doing this, then turn into long strokes
- Finish by letting one finger glide along the spine from the neck down the back, then hold the tail and stroke the entire length. Finish the exercise quietly and slowly

The effect

Tension around the base of the tail and along its length is dissolved. The tail is an extension of the spine, and nervous and insecure dogs have great potential for tension in this area, as they are permanently tensing their tail to pull it down between their legs. In the worst cases, this extreme muscle tension can cause spinal blockages, and also build up in other areas. Massaging the base of the back warms and relaxes the muscles. Points 2 & 3 help with nervousness and tension in the back.

Point 2, close to the base of the tail (lower of the blue spots) has a generally calming effect. In spite of a law forbidding it, there are still dogs whose tails have been docked, and they can also suffer muscle tension as animals can experience phantom pain in the stump of a limb, just as humans do.

Sound magic

Whenever I use my singing bowls, my dogs and cats are always very interested: they seem drawn by the sounds and vibrations. As some of the singing bowls I use in my therapeutic work are very loud and powerful, I obtained some specially small and lightweight bowls for 'dog sound massage,' which can be placed directly onto a dog that is lying down.

Please note that dogs have a very finely developed sense of hearing, so bear this in mind when using singing bowls and proceed with caution. Consider also that although some sounds may not be audible to humans, dogs can certainly hear them. Small singing bowls sometimes have a very high and unpleasant sound. Not all dogs like these high-pitched, high-intensity sounds.

- Invite your dog to get comfortable on the relaxation blanket. (It's advisable to administer a stroking or grooming massage session first to ensure that she is well relaxed and happy to remain lying down)
- Carefully position yourself with a singing bowl near the dog, and tap the bowl very carefully. If the dog doesn't like the sound because it is too intense or too loud, stop immediately You can use the singing bowls in different ways:
- Take a singing bowl in your hand and tap it lightly against the other hand (you can also move it over your dog's body (not touching the dog) to 'distribute' the sound)
- Or, place the singing bowl some distance away from your dog and then tap the bowl

Various sizes of singing bowl.

If you can see that your dog is comfortable and likes the sound, you can then take a lightweight singing bowl (suited to the size of your dog), and place it on the dog's body. The bowl really does need to be a light one!

The effect

In order to communicate how a singing bowl has a positive effect, Peter Hess, author of *Sound Massage according to Peter Hess*, described this effect in a very vivid way: "If you drop a stone into a pool, it creates concentric waves that spread right across the surface. Every molecule of the water is set in motion. The same kind of process happens in the body during a sound massage. The beneficial vibrations are transferred to the body, and spread out in concentric waves – a massage for every cell in the body."

The gentle and very harmonious sounds absorbed by the ear quickly induce a feeling of deep relaxation, whilst the sound waves spread throughout the body. They are perceived as pleasant vibrations and are deeply relaxing, creating a feeling of wellbeing. (Try them yourself first!) Blockages apparently dissolve and energy can flow freely again.

Tip

Before you acquire a singing bowl, make sure you try one out to see if your dog likes the sounds. First practise tapping the singing bowl:

* when it is standing on your palm
* when it is on the floor, and
* when it is on your or another person's body, which should help you avoid harsh rattling noises and become used to handling the bowl

You can use several singing bowls one after the other, but always take care to stay in physical contact with your dog. Keep watching him to see that he is still enjoying the sounds.

It is said that smaller singing bowls, which make a higher sound, have a stronger effect on the head area. The medium-sized ones work on the centre of the body, and the large, deeper-sounding bowls have a more intense effect on all areas. Anyone who is very sensitive in the head area and tends towards tension here may find the higher tones unpleasant. (Very active children often avoid the higher sounds, and are attracted by the lower ones.) So with dogs and their very acute sense of hearing, it is particularly important to be cautious. Which beater to use on the singing bowls is also crucial: the felt beaters are more muted than the rubber or wooden versions.

Every creature has a unique reaction to every sound, so there are no 'standard operating instructions' for using these bowls with a dog.

Energy lines

Stroking the surface of the body in the direction of the flow of the meridians can stimulate the flow of energy.

To achieve this, I recommend stroking the two main meridians and the bladder meridian (see following text).

Brain and pelvic energy lines
The only special meridians (brain (LG) pelvis (KG)) are always in a state of flux, and form something akin to a central axis of the body, running down the front and the back, divided into the brain line and pelvis line. The beneficial influences of these special meridians include harmonisation of the central nervous system, and calming of internal disquiet.

Brain meridian LG

Location: The brain meridian begins between the genitals and the anus, and runs up the spine, over the head to the top lip.

Stroking massage: Directly on the spine from the tail to the head. Draw your thumb or forefinger gently your dog's spine (red line in photo). Repeat this movement 2-3 times. This will stimulate the energy flow of the meridian.

The effect

The brain meridian preserves the body's equilibrium. Veterinarian Dr Draehmpaehl describes its function as follows: "It monitors and regulates the 6 yang meridians, thereby having a harmonising effect on all organs, areas at the back of the body and functions of the central nervous system." Massage strokes along this meridian can therefore assist the central nervous system, and have a soothing effect, as well as being beneficial for the back.

Pelvic meridian KG

Location: The pelvic meridian (KG) runs from the genitals up a central line to the lower jaw.

Stroking massage: From the abdomen to the neck. Draw your thumb or forefinger along the central line running from your dog's abdomen to his neck. Repeating this stroke 2-3 times will stimulate meridian energy.

The effect

The pelvic meridian influences the 6 yin meridians, and is the counterpart to the brain meridian. It is also described as the 'receptive part of the energy.' According to acupressure trainer, Michael Gach, points KG 5-18 of the pelvic meridian (on the stomach) assist in dealing with general physical tension, and enable relaxation. On male dogs, start from KG 6, as shown in the photo on page 122-23. The special points KG 6 and 17 are mentioned in more detail in the section on 'Magic points.'

Bladder meridian

The bladder meridian has more stimulation points on it than the other meridians. According to Gach, it has a very important protective function, as most mental and physical tension collects there. This meridian also represents a connection to the vegetative nervous system from the sexual organs and the urinary tract. The body is cleansed by the excretion of urine. The many points of the bladder meridian which are found on the back take care of energy balance in the internal organs, which may be the reason that insecure and nervous dogs are particularly fond of having these points stimulated, and seem to really enjoy it.

Only the area along the spine is important for the stroking energy line massage – see photo opposite.

The massage is best done with your dog standing. Position yourself beside or behind her and begin to stroke along the paired bladder meridian (see photo opposite). Stroking massage: Draw one thumb at a time or both thumbs at the same time from the neck to the rear of your dog, along the lines directly next to the spine. If you want, you can also make small, gentle circling movements with your thumbs, thus moving from top to bottom in a caterpillar-like motion; repeat 2-3 times.

You can also use the forefinger and middle finger of one hand to draw two lines along the meridian, as this splits into two strands in the upper neck area.

Paired bladder meridian: Red line = governing vessel, blue line = bladder meridian.

Dog Relax

The effect

The bladder meridian starts from the inner corner of each eye, travels up over the base of the nose, the head and the neck, and then splits into two lines running parallel to each other, which travel down along the sides of the spine, reunite on each side of the animal's rear end, and finish in the paws. When the 'nerve exit points' on the back are massaged gently or the line is stimulated by stroking, this has the same effect as massaging the ends of the nerves. Gentle stroking stimulates the connection points, known as 'shu points,' the internal organs and their functions, as well as the dog's neurolymphatic zones, and quickly induces a feeling of wellbeing. 'Shu points' are associated points which are positioned exclusively on the branch of the bladder meridian closest to the spine. They convey energy to the organs.

Some dogs love this massage – and some humans do, too!

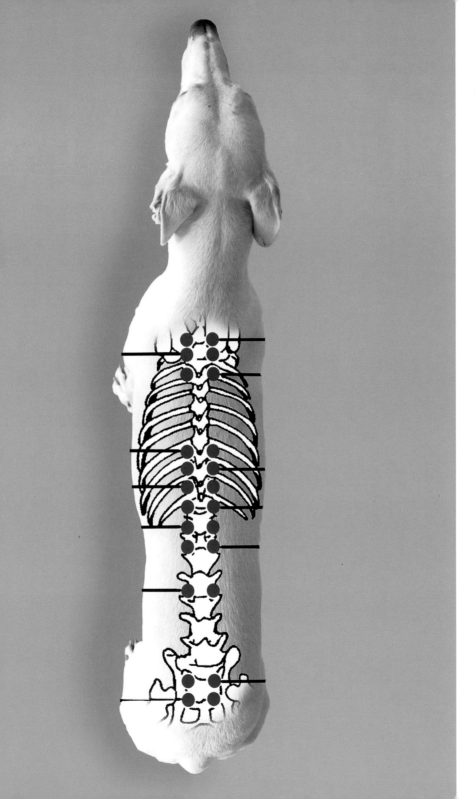

The red spots denote
organ connection points
on the bladder meridian.

Intensive massage

To round off, here's a suggestion for an intensive massage, which is a combination of the various massages described in this book.

Get comfortable with your dog.

- Begin by lightly stroking the dog's neck
- Then stroke your dog's head with circular movements, and touch the magic points
- Gently massage the ear (ear massage)
- Now begin to massage the whole of the neck. Lightly knead the lower neck area (relaxed neck massage). Most dogs will now be relaxed enough to want to lie down
- Massage along your dog's spine (not directly on the spine) from his neck to his rear end. If you can feel your dog's muscles, you can also do some gentle kneading (not with a Greyhound, as they have too little fat)
- Stroke along the spine (bladder meridian massage)
- Massage the area around the base of the tail firmly but gently, and roll the tail gently three times (mood barometer)
- Stroke the legs down to the paws. Massage the paws (fit and healthy on four paws: see page 128)
- If he hasn't done so already, your dog will certainly be relaxed enough to lie down now. Let your hands glide along each side of his body (flowing hands)
- Stroke three times from the head to the end of the tail (including gently rolling the tail) to gently and quietly end the session

The effect

Induces deep relaxation and a feeling of wellbeing; has very complex effects, as described in the sections on the individual massages.

Tip

You have read about various elements of wellbeing massage in the preceding chapters; now be creative and blend together the exercises that your dog likes best. You can massage your dog any time – sitting, lying or standing – whatever suits at that point.

Massage for when you're out and about

Ears

In spite of all the different types of canine ears, the technique for massaging them is the same.

Massage the ears on an alternating basis. Let the ear glide gently between your thumb and your fingers, whilst lightly massaging every part of the ear. To begin with, I would recommend long, gliding strokes with your thumb from the auricle to the edge of the ear. Make light circling movements in the

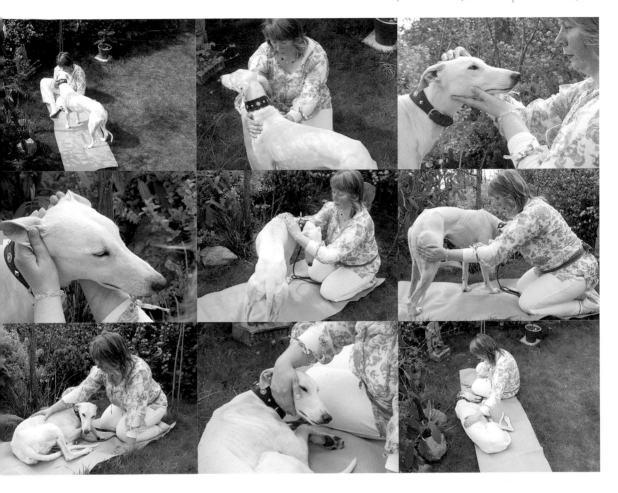

Notes on the photos
This series of photos was taken in spring 2008, and show how a very traumatised dog (in poor physical condition) entrusts himself to me for a massage for the first time. The various touching sequences slowly dissolve the extreme physical tension and fear that he feels, he visibly enjoys being touched, and lies down of his own volition and with complete confidence.

middle of the ear. Also, stroke along the edge of the ear. If your dog has very sensitive ears, you will need to introduce him to this type of massage very slowly. As always, be patient.

Tip

If your dog likes having his ears touched, bend your forefinger and use the joint to carefully stroke the area around the auricle; this is ecstasy for some dogs!

The effect

According to traditional Chinese medicine, there are about 200 acupuncture points on the ear. The ear massage described above is based on the auriculotherapy developed by French doctor Paul Nogier, who believes that the ear represents the body's organs and their functions. Following Nogier's discovery of these ear points, veterinary medicine has also become interested in this subject. Key contributions in this area have been made by Christiane and Dr Hartmut Krüger on the subject of auricular acupuncture on animals. Gentle massage stimulates the ear and, with it, the dog's entire body. The auricular zones exhibit a neural connection with the brain and the spinal cord, which is why ear massage very quickly calms and relaxes. In my experience, this can be put to very positive use to combat anxiety; ear massage is also a helpful tool in assisting your dog to cope with extreme stress.

Tip

Whenever dogs are under stress – whether because of an unfamiliar situation, at the vet's, or after an assignment (working dogs) – it is beneficial to them to have their ears massaged. During this massage, some dogs are absolutely transfixed, they seem to enjoy it so much.

Tip for humans

Incidentally, ear massage has the same effect on humans as it does on dogs of relaxing the entire body and aiding concentration.

I find ear massage to be an important tool in relaxing excited dogs. Here's an example:
I was able to use ear massage to help my young Podenco get over some uncertainties. For his first contact with cows, I took the flustered young dog past the field which contained them a couple of times. Once he had become a little more familiar with these strange animals, I got him to sit and began to massage both his ears. His excitement subsided, the nervous barking stopped, and he simply sat and watched the cows, which had by now approached the fence.

Ear massage has been a great help to me when my dogs have been insecure, excited or anxious. You don't need any special equipment for this simple massage, and you can do it discreetly at any time.

Four different types of ear: Greyhound, Podenco, Labrador cross, Bassett Hound.

Dog Relax

Fit and healthy on four paws

Dogs can be very ticklish or very sensitive on their paws. Some have an aversion to having their claws cut, and therefore a negative association with having their paws touched. If this is the case with your dog, be very careful initially when you begin to touch his paws. Take hold of one paw quite firmly for a short time, and praise your dog and give her a treat for allowing you to do this. Gradual touching of her paws may alleviate her anxiety, but never force the issue.

Keep practicing regularly and patiently until you feel that your dog gives you her paw with complete confidence.

This exercise is best done with your dog lying down in a relaxed state; see photo sequence on pages 131/132 for clarification.

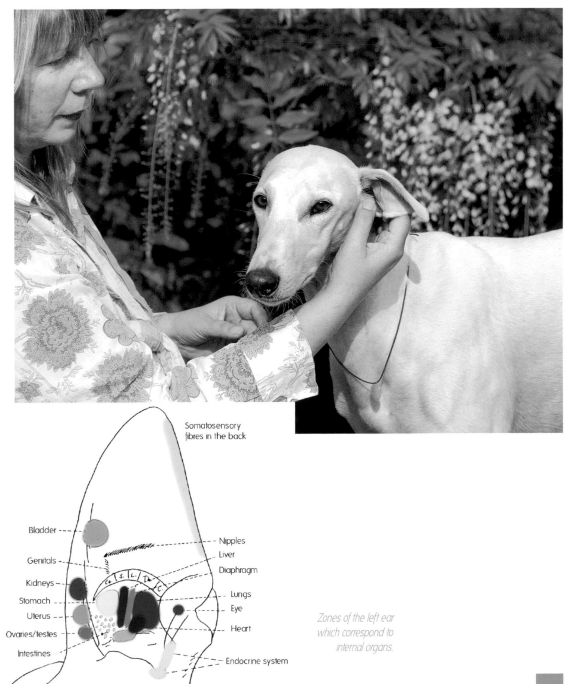

Somatosensory
fibres in the back

Bladder

Genitals

Kidneys

Stomach

Uterus

Ovaries/testes

Intestines

Nipples

Liver

Diaphragm

Lungs

Eye

Heart

Endocrine system

*Zones of the left ear
which correspond to
internal organs.*

129

DOG RELAX

Benji is enjoying an ear
massage, and Santino
is massaging Jio, the
cat's, ear.

Gently massage your own ears. Then stroke them from the
inside to the outside, as if you want to 'unroll' the edge of
your ear. The human body 'lies' in the ear.

- Start with a front leg, and gently stroke it all over 2-3 times from the top down to the paw
- Now take her paw in your hand, and, with your other hand, stroke the paw, toes and claws. Stroke the inside and outside of each claw; also stroke between the metatarsal and between the pads. Imagine you have never before held a dog's paw in your hand and you want to completely explore every inch of this one
- Then move onto the underside of the paw and gently massage the pads with your thumb; some dogs enjoy more pressure here, particularly if they are ticklish! (You can use a special paw care lotion here)
- To finish, stroke 2-3 times from the paw up the leg to stimulate lymph drainage (You will also be massaging the neurolympathic areas on the legs)
- Repeat steps 1-4 with each leg/paw

The effect
There are reflex points on a dog's paws, just as there are on human feet. If you've experienced a reflexology massage – or even just a foot massage – you will know how pleasant and relaxing this can be.

Provided that your dog is happy to be touched, she will really enjoy this massage, which will quickly relax her to the extent that she may even fall asleep.

Tip
Sometimes the paw massage works miracles on very restless dogs. In these cases, it can be helpful

ONE

TWO

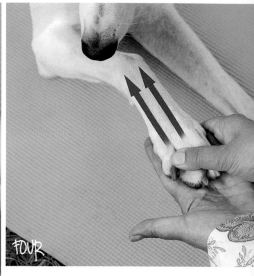

FOUR

THREE

to use firmer strokes from the legs to the paws, and then to massage the paws, or simply hold them and apply light pressure. Stroking or holding the paws causes the dog to focus there, which can enable a stressed dog to quickly become calm. Although every dog reacts differently, I would recommend trying this as I have had very good results with this approach.

Tip for humans
A foot massage on the various reflex zones also has a very relaxing effect on humans, in very active children, imparting a calming and 'grounding' effect.

NATURAL DOG RELAX
Fit for nature – dogs know what's good for them
Every dog feels on top of the world when he is allowed to run around outdoors. Small tree trunks are just asking to be jumped over; different types of surfaces stimulate a dog's sense of perception; balancing on walls helps develop

a sense of balance, and going up and down hills or mountains builds muscle power. Running freely with other dogs doesn't just help build muscle, but also overall fitness and mobility.

If you have a dog that loves water, then let him play in it! Moving in water does a dog as much good as it does a human, and is just as good for the dog's joints. Walking in water or swimming gently trains the muscles, but it is important that both air and water temperatures are not too cold.

Running through sand or mud (please let your dog have some fun!) is another special sort of fitness training – as is digging.

Let your dog be just a dog from time to time; allow him to experience his natural fitness potential and you will have a completely relaxed and happy dog.

Simple, natural relaxation
Dogs just love to relax.

Cuddle time
A simple cuddle is an important feel-good factor for both human and dog.

I am certain that most dog owners love their dogs dearly, but not all of them understand their generic needs.

Have you relaxed yet today ...?

Running, swimming, and digging in mud is something dogs really enjoy!

Dog Relax

About the author

As a psychotherapeutic naturopath; yoga teacher, trained in clinical psychomotor issues; animal psychologist, and dog behaviour counsellor, I have shared my knowledge and my conclusions with you in this book.

Dog Relax is based on my many years of experience. I have invested a great deal of time and energy in this project, and, in so doing, been prepared to go along with new ideas, but have never disregarded the basic science.

Give your intuition some freedom; learn to pay attention to your gut feeling. As Albert Einstein said "Knowledge restricts but imagination knows no bounds."

I wish you much joy with your dog.

DOG RELAX

BIBLIOGRAPHY

Acupuncture Atlas
Deutscher Taschenbuchverlag 2001

Sensory integration and the child
Ayres, Jean A, Springer Verlag 1998

The Learning Gym
Ballinger, Erich, Knauer Verlag 1995

Why I feel what you feel
Bauer, Joachim, Heyne Verlag 2006

The emotional lives of animals
Bekoff, Marc, Animal Learn Verlag 2008

The Pizza Dogs
Bloch, Günther, Kosmos Verlag 2007

I feel, therefore I am
Damasio, Antonio, Ullstein Verlag 2002

Looking for Spinoza: joy, sorrow and the feeling brain
Damasio, Antonio, List Verlag

Your body doesn't lie
Diamond, John, VAK Freiburg, 1995

Acupuncture dogs and cats
Draehmpaehl, Dr D; Zohmann, A, Enke Verlag, 1998

Acupuncture points in the dog
Draehmpaehl, Dr D; Mitzkus & Chr Enke Verlag, Stuttgart

Basic principles of comparative behavioural research
Eibl-Eibesfeldt, Irenäus, Piper Verlag 1999

Qui Gong for me
Engel, Siegbert, blv Verlag, 2009

Dog psychology
Feddersen-Petersen, Dr Dorit Urd, Kosmos Verlag, 2004

Healing points
Gach, Michael Reed, Knaur Verlag, 1992

ACU Yoga
Gach, Michael, Kösel Verlag, 1985

Crystal Healing: The Complete Handbook
Gienger, Michael, Im Osterholt Verlag, 1997

Animals in Translation
Grandin, Temple, Ullstein Verlag, 2007

Singing bowls for health and inner harmony
Hess, Peter, Südwest Verlag, 2007

Complete pain therapy for dogs and cats
Kasper, Zohann A, Sonntag Verlag, 2007

Man meets dog
Lorenz, Konrad, dtv, 2004

ABC of body language
Molcho, Samy, Heinrich Hugendubel Verlag, 2006

Humans need animals
Olbrich, Prof Dr E; Otterstedt, Dr C
Kosmos Verlag, 2003

Gemstone therapy for pets
Quast, Carolin, Sonntag Verlag, 2007

The Little Prince
Saint-Exupery, Antoine de, Karl Rauch Verlag, 1998

Talking to each other
Schultz von Thun, Friedemann, Reinbeck 1998

Dog language
Schöning, Dr Barbara, Kosmos Verlag, 2004

Gemstone therapy for dogs
Stark, Michaela, Aquamarin Verlag, 2007

The healing power of laughter
Titze, Michael, Kösel Verlag, 2001

Taking dogs seriously
Trumler, Eberhard, Piper Verlag, 2004

The essence of the dog
Weidt, Heinz; Berlowitz, Diana, Augustus Verlag, 2001

Pragmatics of human communication
Watzlawick, Paul; Beavin, Janet H; Jackson, Don D, Huber, 1969

The dog
Ziemen, Erik, Goldmann Verlag, 1992

Credits
Diagrams of the ear: Aural acupuncture points by Günter Lange (1985), from the work by Christiane and Dr Hartmut Krüger *Aurikolaakupunktur am Tier*, page 245

Outline diagram of the ear: Ewa Sattarzadeh/ S Pilguj

KG/LG/Bladder taken from *Acupuncture points on the dog* (*Akupunkturpunkte des Hundes*) Dr med vet habil Dirk Draehmpaehl, page 143

Photo credits
Tanja Askani: pg 9, middle; Jude Brooks: pg 29, 33, 83, top, 87: Paul Castle: pg 55; Ulla Eugelink: pg 86, 88; Nea Hinz: pg 106; Dorit Krausen: pg 17; MEV-Verlag pg 3, 15, 46, 50-51, 80, 85, 100-101, 126-127 ; Christiane Michels, DUO Ibiza: pg 45, 83, bottom, 137; Karin Müller, Die Bergischen Tierfreunde eV: pg 84; Heike Reiss: pg 89, top; Yvonne Schmitz: pg 9, left, 42; Edelgard Westenberger: pg 89, bottom.

All other photos and photo montages by Ricardo Pilguj.

1-845843-35-9 £12.99*

1-845843-22-9 £12.99*

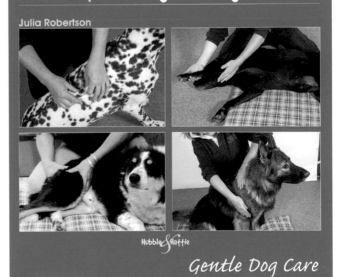

Gentle Dog Care

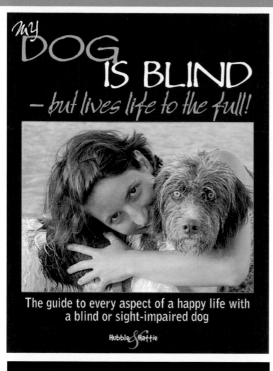
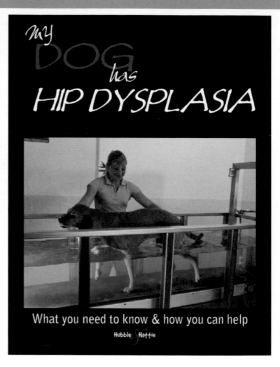

1-845843-80-9 £9.99

Dog Cookies

healthy allergen-free treat recipes for your dog

Martina Schöps

Hubble & Hattie

Christiane Blenski

Dog Games

Stimulating play to entertain your dog and you

Hubble & Hattie

1-845843-32-8 £15.99

Clever Dog! 1-845843-45-8 £12.99*

Waggy tails & wheelchairs 1-845842-92-5 £12.99*

Smellorama 1-845842-93-2 £9.99*

Dinner with Rover 1-845843-13-7 £9.99

Walkin' the dog 1-845841-02-7 £4.99*

Know your dog 1-845840-72-3 £9.99*

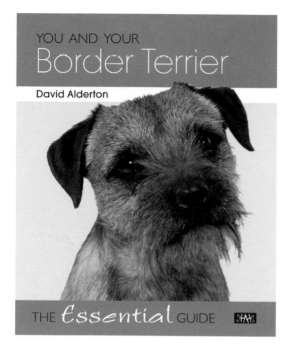
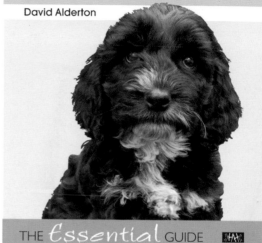
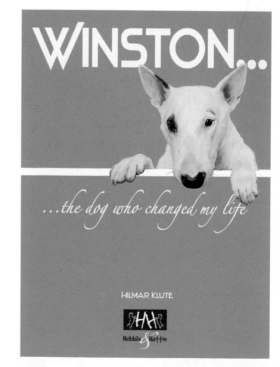